Way
of the
Positive Flow

by

Lawrence Vijay Girard

(Nayaswami Vijay)

FruitgardenPublishing

"Information and Inspiration
for Living in Harmony with Life"

First Printing 2010
Way of the Positive Flow
Revised Edition

ISBN 0-9646457-8-5
EAN-13: 9780964645783

To truth seekers everywhere.

To my spiritual family
who have helped me to realize
more of life's mysteries then
I ever could have hoped for.

Contents

Contents

Chapter 1
So, What do I do Now?

A movie was once made about a man who ran for public office. He was such a long shot for the job that he didn't pay much attention to what he would do if he got elected. Instead, he concentrated on saying the things that he thought would best get him there. In the end, all of his efforts to get elected were successful. At the closing of the movie he completed his victory speech, turned to his aide and asked with uncertainty in his voice, "So, what do I do now?"

How often it is in life that we express those same sentiments to ourselves: So, what do I do now?

We wake up every morning to face untold numbers of expected and unexpected experiences. Much of the time we do not have a clue what the right thing to do is. Maybe if we knew what was coming next we could plan things out. As it happens, even when we do know the basics of what the future holds for us we don't always react in the best possible way. Most of the time, we have no idea what is coming next. So...What do I do now?

It amazes me that we can go through years of familial, educational and societal indoctrination and still be totally unclear about how to live successfully in this world. Even most religious training leaves vast gaps in our understanding about how to cope with the ups and downs, ins and outs, of

1

daily life. All too many of us grow up without knowing how to find practical workable solutions to the challenges that we face every day - to say nothing of figuring out how to be dynamically happy.

As children we are given lists of do's and don'ts to memorize. DO look both ways when you cross the street. DON'T wipe your hands on your pants. DO say thank you. DON'T chew with your mouth open. As we get older the list gets longer and harder to manage because life isn't as simple as up or down, right or wrong. The basic tenets that we live by make sense most of the time, yet we all have strayed from our personal list of do's and don'ts at different times in our lives. So how can we live with ourselves when this happens? Have we failed our parents, our teachers and ourselves? Or are there times when wrong is right? Or at least okay?

It certainly can be confusing.

In life there are countless situations for which there is no list of do's and don'ts to follow. What list tells us how to act when we get fired from a job? What do we do when our car stalls in the middle of the freeway during rush hour traffic and we are late for an appointment? How do we choose the right treatment, or lack of treatment, for a dying parent or child? Should we or shouldn't we, take a new job, buy a new house, get married or make any other choice in life. How do we deal with all of the uncertainties that life will bring us and make decisions that we can feel good about? And on a more subtle level, how do we come to grips with the countless thoughts and impulses that stream through our minds each day in a way that will bring us peace of mind, rather than the hopelessness we feel when complete fulfillment seems always to be just out of reach?

Millions of people go to psychics, psychologists and prophets each day to find solutions to the challenges that life presents them. For some, it is a genuine call for help at a time of need. For others, it may be an attempt to find an easy way out.

So, What do I do Now?

In all cases, people are saying in some way, "So, what do I do now?"

As a teenager I spent many hours floating along the shores of California on a surfboard. While my purpose for being out on the water was to ride waves, I found that much of the time I was just sitting out there watching the forces of nature do their thing in the sky, on the land and in the water. While I was waiting for a wave to ride I would study the way all of nature seemed to interact in harmony. I took this observation to heart as I rode the waves. I tried to move in harmony with them, to be a natural part of them, the way a fish swims in the sea or a bird flies in the air.

Over the years I found this approach to surfing entering into the rest of my life. I began to see that flowing with the energies of my experiences on land was not all that different from riding waves on the ocean.

Most of us have been trained to approach life in a very linear fashion. We analyze the problem, come up with a list of possible solutions, give each possibility a value, and then add or subtract to find the correct action. While this may work with accounting it doesn't come anywhere close to dealing with human relationships or the countless internal struggles that we each wrestle with on a daily basis.

What we need in order to deal with life properly is a way of finding solutions that takes into consideration not only the things that we know about, but also factors that we may not be aware of. This system of evaluation must take into account the best interests of all involved in any given situation. It will also need to take into account our personal capabilities. The solution for one person in any given situation will not always be the same as for another person in the same situation.

When I first started to explore the idea of consciously riding the wave of my life I thought that I was walking in uncharted territory. As I began to actively search for a greater understanding of the subject I found that this was not the case.

3

Way of the Positive Flow

From time immemorial people have sought to harmonize their individual lives with the forces of life itself.

The most common word that the English language uses to describe these efforts is religion. As I read about the various religions of the world I found that each one thought that they were the one and only true way. To follow their true way you had to follow their true list of do's and don'ts and believe that their leader was the only true leader.

As I mentioned earlier, lists of do's and don'ts will not give us the kind of guidance that we need to be successful in life. Only one true leader doesn't cut it either. Common sense tells us that an eternal God would not come to only one group of people during just one time in history. Doesn't it seem a bit self-serving when someone claims that their way is the only way? When do they say we will get proof of their "only true way"? When we are gone from this world and can't come back to tell others whether it is true or not. We need help here and now, not just in the future.

These exclusionary philosophies of unseen future rewards made me gag. I just couldn't swallow them. So, I dug a little deeper. Instead of reading about religions I began to read about the lives of those who have been recognized by many as being successful at living life in the best possible way: the saints of all religions.

As I studied the lives of great souls from many different times and religious backgrounds I found something that surprised me. None of them ever preached in a sectarian way. Their disciples might have, but the saints themselves did not. Most importantly, they all said that God - no matter what name we use for God - does exist and that the main purpose of life is to grow towards our own direct experience of that truth. Another thing that I found was that none of the saints, to the best of my knowledge, ever said, "Take my word for it!" They were much more likely to have said, "Don't take my word for it, realize it for yourself!"

So, What do I do Now?

The thing that convinced me to take the inspiration of their lives seriously is the way that they live. The saints surf the energies of their lives with a poise, wisdom, love and joy that we all feel instinctively drawn to. Even without the concept of God they show the truly wondrous potential that we all have.

As I studied the teachings that sit at the foundation of all great traditions I found that there are underlying truths that all paths follow. I began to realize that differences between these traditions address issues pertinent to the time and place that a particular saint was present, rather than representing a difference in the underlying truths.

The underlying principles that unite all paths form the heart of the *Way of the Positive Flow*. No matter what your religious background or lack thereof, you will find that the application of these ideas and techniques will bring new dimensions of perception and understanding to you. Every aspect of this approach towards life can be personally verified by anyone who applies its precepts.

The *Way of the Positive Flow* does not represent a "new breakthrough" in the art of living. It is simply a fresh expression of a time tested approach that aligns our efforts with the way life itself is made. I invite you to put these ideas to the test in your own life and see for yourself if they are true.

Chapter 2
The Positive Flow

In order to approach living our lives in the best possible way we need to understand what we are working with. Is life just a biological accident gone out of control? Are we simply the sum total of our genetic markers? Or is there some larger picture into which all of the smaller definitions of life can fit as parts of the whole?

There are two basic approaches to answering this question. One approach is to look at life from the outside in, the way a scientist does. The other is to look at life from the inside out, the way a saint does. Interestingly enough, with the recent advances in scientific understanding they both have come to the same conclusion: Life is not what it appears to be! The creation that we experience outside of ourselves - through the senses - is an illusion.

Here are some examples:

Q. Look at any part of your body. Touch it. Slap it. Is it solid?

A. No. It seems solid. Our senses tell us that our bodies are solid like every other "solid" thing in the world. But scientists tell us that our bodies are mostly space. So our impression of solidness is not really true.

Q. Look at the outside of a building. Is it stationary or in motion?

A. It might look solid and at rest, but not only is it whirling through space with the rest of us and our planet, its molecular structure is gyrating all over the place as well.

Complicating our situation even further is the effect that our desires have on our sensory experiences. We seek to be happy through our senses but the logic of doing so does not always lead to the desired result.

Q. If eating cookies makes you happy, why not keep eating them endlessly?

A. Besides the possibility that you will run out of cookies, you will most certainly make yourself sick if you eat too many. So unless having a stomach-ache also makes you happy you can never eat your way to happiness.

So what does all of this mean? It means that our senses and our impulses don't give us a realistic view of what is really going on all around us. Our physcial powers of perception present only a narrow band of the physical world in which we live and give us no view of that which is beyond their capabilities. There is much more to life than we can perceive through the senses. True perception is a function of consciousness, not just the totality of sensory input.

Many scientists have said that consciousness sprang forth spontaneously as the result of biological mutation. This explanation is based on limited techniques which only identify and quantify the physical components present in any given form of life. Just as the scientific ability to see out into space has improved over the years the ability of science to reach into what is called inner space has improved as well. This exploration has led scientists to the very threshold of not only the way life is manifest, but where it comes from. The scientific study of the substructure of life has been documented by Dr. Deepak Chopra. I invite you to explore his writings if you are interested in details of this subject that go beyond the scope of this book.

The really amazing thing is that the conclusions that Dr. Chopra details as a scientist coincide with the explanations

Way of the Positive Flow

of the creation found in the scriptures of India - which were written thousands of years ago. How did those ancient sages come to the same conclusions without the scientific techniques of today? They studied the subject from the inside out, rather than the outside in. Instead of electron microscopes they used the power of the mind to intensely focus their attention within themselves, thus reversing the flow of their consciousness from out into the world to within; towards its source inside their own beings.

Through this inward exploration of consciousness the saints of east and west have plumbed the depths of life's source and its purpose. The saints of all religions have said that the creation is a manifestation of the consciousness of God. While more and more scientists are saying that life has sprung from an infinite consciousness, they do not always give that consciousness a name. In either case, what we end up with is that all of the creation - all of life - comes from and is a part of one infinite consciousness. Therefore, we are all part of that infinite consciousness. The saints say that the only reason we are not aware of our larger infinite Self is because we are using our senses to look outside, rather than using our souls to look inside.

Let me paint a picture of what the arena of life looks like so that we can then utilize our understanding of the way life is made in order to harmonize with it and maximize our efforts.

The creation is like a huge wave that has sprung up from an ocean of infinite unmanifested consciousness. This ocean is not limited to the three dimensional view that our senses provide. God, the ocean of Spirit, is center everywhere, circumference nowhere. The wave of the creation rises out of not only each molecule of the creation but even the space between the molecules. So when I describe life as a wave, it is a wave that springs out simultaneously from...everywhere.

The ocean before the creation is infinite, ever-existing, ever-conscious, ever-new love and joy. This infinite consciousness of true happiness is what our language calls God. God is beyond the creation but has also become the creation.

The thing that makes the wave of life appear separate from the ocean is that the creation is limited: finite. It is the ever-increasing limitations of the creation that distinguish life at the base of the wave from life at the peak. Near the base of the wave life has few limits; consciousness is not far from its infinite beginnings. At the peak of the wave life is very limited.

Life as experienced through the creation starts from its source in the ocean of Spirit as the realm of thought and ideas. This ideational or causal plane is where the soul - individualized Spirit - first becomes identified as separate from the whole. This is where infinite bliss begins to diminish and the soul can express specific thoughts like: "Oh, what the heck, let's spend the next zillion years making a universe over...well....over there. And here is what we will do...."

Next on the journey of increasing limitation is the realm of energy. Energy is fine particles of motion powered by thought. The realm of energy is sometimes referred to as the astral plane. This is where the individualized soul is garbed in a body of energy. It is in the astral body that we store commitments of energy that we have gathered through our countless experiences in the physical world. This energy is colored by the thoughts that animate them, creating a multicolored body of light. The colors of astral body express the consciousness of the soul.

It is in the astral plane that most souls reside before and after experiencing the most distant extension of consciousness into the creation: the physical plane. The astral plane is where the concepts of heaven and hell find their reality - although not in the way that many people are used to thinking. These are not final destinations for an eternal reward or punishment as the result of a single lifetime on planet earth. These are places where we go for a temporary reprieve from the challenges of life in the physical world. Our time in the astral world can be devilishly unpleasant or angelically beautiful.

Way of the Positive Flow

The causal body of thought, covered by the astral body of energy, is what animates the physical body that we live in. The physical creation that we perceive all around us through our senses is at the very peak of the wave of life. It is our complete mental absorption in our physical bodies and in the senses that distracts us from looking inside ourselves to find our source in the ocean of Spirit.

The wave of God's creation that we call life is animated by a great power. This power, having sprung up out of infinite consciousness has caused the creation to flow and extend itself from that which is infinite to that which is finite. This outward flowing force is what keeps the creation going. Fortunately, there is also a flow that is drawing the creation back into the ocean of Spirit. Just as a physical wave goes up and comes down, so it is that the creation also returns to its source after having danced on the canvas of the cosmos.

A key point to understand about these flows of consciousness towards or away from infinite consciousness is that they are consciously active. In India they call these forces prakriti and aprakrit. From a Christian perspective you might say God/Christ and Satan. In Asia many would say Yin and Yang. No matter what we choose to call these natural forces it is important to understand that if we want to improve our lives most productively we need to consciously align ourselves with the flow that is moving towards infinite consciousness. It is on these waves of energy flowing back to our infinite home in Spirit that we want our life to ride.

Why is it important to understand any of this stuff? Here is why. The forces of life that are flowing towards infinite consciousness are the positive flow. That which flows towards limitation is the negative flow. Our alignment to these two flows is the basis for coming up with a value system and strategies for success in life that actually work.

Each day we make choices about how to act. On what do we base these decisions? The issue that ultimately determines what we do in life is the urge to be happy. This primal seeking of happiness can be hidden in many layers of seemingly opposing impulses. As an example: In some cases we want to do the right thing, not just the thing that makes us happy. Sometimes right decisions hurt. The desire to do the right thing in a potentially hurtful situation is a reflection of the deeper kind of happiness that comes from doing right regardless of how we feel about it. In this way, if we were able to follow all of our impulses to their root we would find that they come from the souls yearning to be infinitely loving and joyful.

The soul is made from an ocean of infinite joy and it can never be completely satisfied until it returns to that joy. In our efforts to recapture that distant happiness we have sought fulfillment outside of ourselves through the senses, but in doing so we entangle ourselves in an endless stream of consequences that keep us stuck in this world of limitation.

By aligning our consciousness with the positive flow of life we will find that we have a compass that can lead us through the maze of challenges that we face. Remember, the positive flow is center everywhere and active, always trying to help us move forward toward ultimate happiness. It is with us and available to us wherever we go, no matter what we are doing. All we need to do is develop our ability to tap in to it.

The reason this can work for everybody and in all situations is that the positive flow is directionally based from our current state of consciousness. The solutions that we receive through our attunement to the flow will take into account who we are as individuals and the totality of the situation to which they apply. This is why lists of this is good and that is bad do not really work. That which is good in one situation for one person, might be bad for another person in the same basic situation.

The real basis for making good decisions in life is not as much about where those decisions fit on the cosmic list of ultimate truths, as which direction that decision will point the boat of our consciousness right here and now.

Way of the Positive Flow

Thoughts and actions that expand our horizons are by their nature those which align us with the positive flow. Things that contract us, thus increasing our limitations, are attuned to the negative flow. It is our attunement to the positive or negative flows in life that determine how we are doing and where we are going. It is through our awareness of these inward flows that we can tune in to and validate the correctness of our thoughts, actions and decisions.

Most people just bob on the surface of life, allowing the waves of circumstance to throw them around, giving up any idea of control over their happiness and their future. By consciously attuning ourselves to the positive flow we can alter the course of our lives and consciously determine the quality of our future. This doesn't mean that everything will always be peaches and cream! But just like a surfer, the more waves you ride the better you get at it. The more time we spend consciously attuning ourselves to the positive flow of life, the better we will get at it. The results that we see will not be theoretical. They will be validated through our own personal experience.

When you live in tune with the positive flow your life will take on a kind of synchronicity that will amaze you. You will find yourself in the right place at the right time so that the right things can happen for you. This will happen so often that you will wonder how you ever got along before. Then you will remember that you didn't always get along so well!

Chapter 3
Energy, Magnetism &
the Three Qualities

Have you ever dropped a pebble into a pool of water and watched the ripples that flow out from where the pebble entered the water? Have you ever wondered what the ripples that flow out are made of? They appear to be water but what they actually are is energy flowing through the water. All of life is animated by energy that flows underneath the surface of what we can perceive through our senses and it is thought which puts those underlying energies into motion.

If we want to turn on the light in a room we first do it as a thought. We put that idea into motion by sending energy through the body to turn on the switch. Moving the switch causes energy to flow through the wire which activates the light. The light then flows as energy to our eyes. That light is then translated into electrical impulses in the brain and we think: the light is on.

This is how all of life works; the way life is made. All flows of energy in life are activated by underlying thoughts. By understanding how this works we can utilize this knowledge to achieve any goals that we might have in life.

This includes the larger goal of reuniting our souls with the ocean of Spirit, as well as the achievement of smaller goals in every part of life. Understanding that it is the underlying energy that we want to work with is key to grasping how we are

13

going to apply the creative potential of the universal positive flow to our lives.

Once we realize that it is energy we are working with we can move on to the amount of energy that we have available to us and how to focus that energy in the direction of our goals. In terms of how much energy is available to us, ultimately there is no limit. As parts of the whole we have the potential to draw on the whole. In practice, we haven't yet realized our oneness with the whole so the amount of energy that we can draw on will be determined by how effective we are in attuning ourselves to the positive flow. Suffice it to say, there is plenty of energy available if we are willing to take the time to learn how to draw on it.

The way that we draw upon the energies of the positive flow is a little different then the way most people are used to thinking. We are used to thinking in terms of plugging into wall sockets with extension cords or attaching a hose to a spigot. While these analogies do work to a certain degree in terms of plugging into the positive flow, there is a much more subtle aspect of the situation that I want to share with you. It has to do with the principles of magnetism.

Wherever energy exists there is a magnetic field radiating out from that energy. Let's use the example of an electromagnet to help us understand how this works. Have you ever seen one of those big electromagnets that are used at auto dismantlers to lift up old cars? It is a big piece of metal attached to a high powered extension cord which is raised and lowered on a big crane.

What is all of that electricity for? How does it work? The metal without electricity flowing through it is not a powerful magnet. The reason is that all of the molecules of the metal, each with its own power of magnetic attraction, are facing in different directions and in effect canceling each other out. When you turn on the electricity a large flow of energy causes all of the individual molecules to line up in the same direction and

14

work as a team. With everyone lined up and working together, as you increase the flow of electricity you can create a force powerful enough to pick up thousands of pounds.

This analogy brings up several points of interest to our discussion:

- Like attracts like. When you turn on this powerful magnet it attracts other metal objects. It doesn't attract plastic, rubber or anything else that isn't metal.
- A strong magnetism overcomes the powers of a weak magnetism. This applies to both drawing or repelling other energies.
- A strong flow of energy is what causes the molecules to line up and increase their magnetism. Conversely, when energies are low or scattered there is little magnetism.
- Since all of life is energy, each part of life has its own magnetism and the quality of that magnetism is unique to that particular expression of life.

This concept that "like attracts like" is very important to understanding how we can utilize the positive flow for an overall improvement in the quality of our lives, as well as the ability to manifest specific results. Our individual consciousness represents the energies that we are putting out towards life, whatever we are radiating will attract more of the same. If our thoughts and actions are negative, we will attract negative experiences. If we radiate positive energies, positive things will come our way. While it is true that "negative" things do happen sometimes to "positive" people, it is also true that they are much less likely to happen. It is also true that positive people find positive perspectives within experiences that others might consider negative.

One of the reasons that negative things can happen to positive people is that a strong negative magnetism can be more powerful than a weak positive power to resist. Why is it that one person survives an airplane crash and another doesn't? How is it that one person avoided the crash through a series of unexpected incidents? The world is made up of an incredibly complex interaction of individual energies that are all connected through the powers of magnetism. If our own positive energies are strong we are much more likely to succeed in our efforts. If our energies are scattered we weaken our chances of success.

The power to repel is also a part of magnetism. When our own energies are strongly charged, weaker energies are not able to affect us. If something negative is strong enough to reach us, the results will not be as bad as they would have been if we were weak to begin with. This is why some people can be around others who are ill and not get the disease themselves. It isn't just an issue of anti-bodies. The power of consciousness to magnetically repel negative energies is one of our greatest protections in life. This is actually how the body's immune responses are activated - by the positive magnetic power of repulsion.

This brings us to an extremely important point: Every part of life is magnetic, since it is a manifestation of energy, and the quality of magnetism that it radiates is unique unto itself. These magnetic patterns range from the most simple in the minerals to the most complex in human beings.

These patterns also apply to flows of energy beyond individual life forms. They effect everything from today's weather, the stock market, scientific discovery, musical trends, governments, and on and on, all the way up to the exploding of stars and the creation of galaxies. They reach to the very roots of the process of creation and dissolution of all that is separate from the ocean of Spirit.

We have all heard it said that no two snowflakes are the same. It is the same with all of life. Every part of the creation is unique. We may not be able to perceive this uniqueness with our senses, but it is there. This uniqueness is actually a great help to us. If we could perceive the magnetism radiating from all of life around us we would have the ability to tell if that energy is in tune with the positive or negative flow for us.

Energy, Magnetism & the Three Qualities

Keep in mind that each person must walk their own path in life. That which is a step backward for one may be a step forward for someone else. Learning to read the magnetic patterns, or vibrations, of any given thing, person or situation is not about being judgmental, but is essential for learning to discriminate between that which will expand our horizons and be beneficial to us or that which will contract our awareness and close us off from our highest potential. This is one of the secret arts of living in the positive flow. When we develop our ability to internally perceive what the vibrations around us are saying, we will have the information that can best guide us in making good decisions about what to do.

It is said in India that all of life is made of three qualities: That which is elevating, activating or downward-pulling. Elevating qualities are expressions of the positive flow. Downward-pulling qualities express the negative flow. Activating qualities can lead in either direction depending on how they are used.

Remember earlier when we talked about expanding and contracting consciousness as the broader guideline from which to view our lives? Elevating qualities expand us. They are expressions of and attune us to the positive flow. Beautiful places, food vital with life force, beautiful flowers and their scents, cleanliness of body and mind, cheerfulness, the inclination to help others, peace, love and compassion are all examples of that which is elevating in life.

Some downward-pulling qualities are: selfishness, laziness, a filthy dwelling, food that is over cooked or not fresh, swearing, places where evil deeds have been committed, jealousy or vengefulness. These qualities contract our consciousness. They bind us to the limited confines of the ego instead of the universal realm of the soul.

Activating qualities can go in positive or negative directions. Over-chattiness about generally pleasant subjects is a positive activating expression, while speaking constantly about unpleasant subjects is a negative direction. Use of the martial arts to improve oneself and help others is a positively activating endeavor. Using the martial arts to unnecessarily hurt others is a negatively activating energy.

Don't forget, this is not about making a list of all the "right" things to do and the "wrong" things to avoid. In the beginning it can be helpful to list different qualities that you know are representative of the three basic qualities so that you can get a frame of reference. But if we stop at making a list we will be missing the deeper purpose of our efforts. It is essential that we learn to recognize the vibrations of things in and around us from an inner sense of knowing. Then it will be like having our own portable radar system.

When your internal system is up and running you will be able to apply these broader concepts to the specifics of where you are as an individual. You will be able to inwardly know if any thing, situation or circumstance is positive or negative for you in that given moment. Remember it is a flow, that which is not so good for today may be fine for tomorrow. You may find that you should avoid a particular type of place or food for years and then find one day that it's now okay for you to go there or eat that.

Being awake and ready is very much a part of living in the positive flow. When our consciousness is energized with attentiveness and enthusiasm - which are elevating qualities -we will get much more out of our life experiences and be more successful at dealing with them. There is literally no limit to how refined this ability to perceive the qualities of life energies within us and around us can become.

The knowledge about life that we can receive from attunement to the positive flow is ours as a birthright. It is part of the way life is made. We don't need to beg for it, we need to open ourselves up to being aware of that which is already present in life all around us. As you develop your ability to inwardly perceive this new information, remember that an open and humble heart is elevating, while egotistical pride is downward-pulling.

The positive flow contains all potential for good. What is good? You might think of the word good as an extension of the word God which is by definition the highest good. So in order to do good in this world, we must be linked to that which God would have us do. How do we know what God wants from us at any given moment? To find out, we attune the radio of our consciousness to the inner broadcast of the positive flow which is the source of all knowledge, all power, and most importantly, all happiness.

Chapter 4
Self-Honesty, Self-Acceptance & Universal Identification

If you were going to construct a new building it wouldn't make much sense to do it on a pool of quicksand. You would look for a site that had firm bedrock beneath it, so that the building could stand strong through the years.

The bedrock of attunement to the positive flow is self-honesty. This is not simply an issue of always telling the truth - an elevating quality. It is about looking within ourselves and being willing to see ourselves as we currently are and not how we wish we were. We need to be able to see how we are expressing the positive and negative qualities of consciousness that are available to us. If we tend to be hot tempered or quick to judge then we need to be willing to admit it to ourselves. If we desire material things that we do not have we need to acknowledge those desires. If we tend to be moody, mentally scattered, selfish, jealous, lazy or any other negative quality, it is essential we recognize that these energies are flowing through us.

At the same time, be sure to take an accounting of your good qualities. Are you cheerful, respectful of others, quick to lend a hand, humble, truthful, hard working, attentive to necessary details, self-controlled or loving? These are just some of the many ways that the positive flow can be expressed. Take a look inside yourself and acknowledge these positive qualities.

Self-Honesty, Self-Acceptance & Universal Identification

One of the things that can keep us from getting a clear look at who we are is the attitude of shame. While intense regret for our mistakes can be an appropriate feeling when we have erred, the kind of shame that keeps us from fully looking at our innermost feelings puts a limit on our ability to move forward. We have all done things that we wish we hadn't done. Or we may be glad we did them even though we knew it wasn't a good thing to do and we are ashamed of that. We may also have feelings that are so private that even we don't like to look at them!

Here are two ideas to keep in mind. The first is that you are not alone. There are billions of people on this planet who all have "stuff" that is just another variation of whatever yours might be. The second thing is that God has been around since the beginning. There isn't anything that God has not seen before. We might put our own little twist to it but in terms of getting into trouble the saying, "There's nothing new under the sun!" applies to anything that we may have done. Shame is just another pseudo claim of the negative flow. It presents a false reason not to move forward.

Shame makes us feel so bad that our energy gets blocked. When we get rid of shame we can stand up and say, "Oh well, I really messed up, but I'm going to turn things around from now on!" So give shame back to the negative flow by releasing it through a positive, humble, openness to God's creation as it is manifesting uniquely through each one of us.

As you evaluate who you are, start by making an accounting of the "positive and negative" ways that you think and act. Try to discern the quality that lies underneath each of the things that you have noticed. Is it elevating, activating or downward-pulling?

This is not about judging yourself. You are just taking inventory of what is there. Try not to blow your positive or negative qualities out of proportion! That isn't honest either. What we are trying to do is see clearly the way different qualities

21

of consciousness flow through us; from our first impulse to the taking of action. This process will help us see the difference between the thoughts and actions themselves, and the qualities of consciousness that caused those thoughts and actions to manifest.

If a person stops on the side of the road to help someone repair a flat tire that could be the expression of a giving nature. But if a man stops to help a woman in the hopes of picking her up, that is a totally different energy underlying the same physical actions.

If we feed and clothe our children out of love for them our attitude is different than if we do it out of a grudging sense of duty. Doing a good job at work for the sake of doing our personal best is different than doing a job well just so we can get a bonus. Although in any of these examples doing the right thing with the wrong attitude is better than doing the wrong thing with a wrong attitude. What we want to do is recognize the underlying types of energy that we are working with so we can begin to consciously improve things.

If a person who had been neglecting their family altogether started taking care of their family even grudgingly, you would pat them on the back for moving in the right direction. This is how we can put an actual value to the decisions that we make in life. Instead of labeling decisions as good or bad we should ask: Which way is this choice taking me? Is it moving me towards a higher, more positive way of expression or is it pulling me down into a deeper pit of loneliness and separateness from the good in life?

You see how it works?

The truth is that most of our actions in life are a mixture of positive and negative energies. Only those who walk through life untouched by the limitations of the ego can act in all circumstances without any selfish motive. Since we can see the world we live in is not filled with saints, we can infer that each of us is more positively charged than some and more negatively charged than others. Exactly where we fit in comparison to others is not really germane to our situation except to the extent that we are affected by the qualities of magnetism that others around us are radiating. By taking this larger view we will alleviate some of the pressure that we might feel about our shortcomings. Remember, improving our lives is not so much about where we are now as which way we are headed and how much energy we are applying towards that direction.

The tendency to compare ourselves to others is in itself a quality of the negative flow. When we do that we distance ourselves from others and add energy to the ego, which by its nature encourages separateness. Try to see all people as your own larger Self manifesting in different ways. This broader view of life also helps us to realize that we are all here in the same boat. As a great sage once said, "Those who are too good for this world are adorning another world."

When we connect ourselves to this expanded perspective we can see that we are actually fulfilling the purpose of God's creation by being here. So accept yourself for whatever role has been given to you to play. No matter where we seem to be in the process of remembering our true universal Self, we are all equal parts of the great story called life.

Most people appraise the value of a person's life by the things that they accomplish outwardly or by the opinions that are held of them by others. The real standard of how one lives is the quality of his/her consciousness and not the specifics of how it manifests. An isolated leper with an open heart can stand closer to the goal of self-realization than a doctor who has saved a thousand lives only for the sake of money.

How does God view all of this?

The saints say that God's view is simpler than we might expect from the creator of life. God simply loves us: no ifs, ands or buts. It does not matter how confused or errant we might become; God always loves us. Of course, God's love for us does not mean that we will not have to experience the consequences

23

of our actions, but it is certainly consoling to know that we will never be cast out into an eternity of suffering. God is always trying to draw us towards infinite love through the forces of the positive flow.

God's view never changes. What happens is that our view changes. As we refine our ability to live in tune with the positive flow we will find that the energies of the negative flow will not interest us. We will begin to feel more and more comfortable working with the underlying energies in life. As greater levels of positive energy are able to flow through us we will hardly notice things that used to cause us great difficulty. Gradually we will reach the stage where living constantly in an awareness of the positive flow will be the most natural thing in the world for us.

Keep in mind that the purpose of this process is not to pick ourselves apart and psychologically wrestle with ourselves. It is about honesty, self-acceptance and the beginnings of re-cognizing ourselves in terms of energy rather than psychology. While it is true that some people need the help of a counselor to get this process going, if it is left on a psychological level the results will have a definite limit.

Take the time to deeply reflect on yourself. Do not just pass this by as something that can be done at some more convenient time in the future. All too often we put important tasks aside thinking: I'll get back to it soon. And then time passes and we never get back to it. This is an example of how the negative flow works its subtle influence in our lives. Little things get in the way of more important things and we do not even notice that time has once again passed us by. There is much to do in this lifetime. Let us hearken to the task!

Chapter 5
Tuning in to the Positive Flow
Part 1

There are three overarching ways to cultivate attunement with the positive flow plus one that binds them all together. They are discrimination, service and love. The one that binds them all together is meditation. The goal is to cultivate a balance of these areas in our lives. When we have achieved that balance we will be firmly planted on the path of wisdom, which is living in complete attunement to the positive flow.

Discrimination

Discrimination starts with intelligence but quickly moves on to more subtle aspects of understanding. There are many people who are very intelligent and have vast intellectual prowess that do not express much wisdom. At the same time, there are wise saints who neither read nor write. So it is helpful to understand that intelligence is not limited to being expressed as intellectual ability or training. Intelligence can be turned towards creatively expressing any aspect of life. A rocket scientist who has a great intellect for engineering may have no clue when it comes to intelligently interacting with people. Likewise, a person with keen insight into the workings of the human mind may have no clue when it comes to fixing a car or building a house.

Intelligence is an elevating quality. It represents an open and expanding awareness. The intellect is the application

25

of intelligence in what is basically an activating direction. The intellect can be taken towards elevating when used for things associated with the positive flow, stay more or less neutrally activating if used just for the sake of using it, or it can be downward-pulling if used to harm oneself or others. Using the mind to solve the riddles of disease would be a positive use of the intellect, while becoming good at board games like chess would be a more or less a neutral use of the intellect. Becoming a clever con man would be a downward-pulling use of the intellect.

The highest use of the intellect is that which helps us and others to live in harmony with the positive flow. Reading the great scriptures of the world is a time honored way to absorb the great truths concerning life. Studying the discoveries of those who have come before us will save us from having to reinvent the wheel each time we explore new levels of understanding.

There is also a more subtle elevating aspect to reading the scriptures. The written word can carry the same vibrational power as the spoken word. When we absorb words that are spoken or written by souls of realization they vibrationally reach out to us and positively magnetize us. This is the more important reason it is so good to read holy writings. It is, in fact, what makes them holy. Along with the meaning of the words, scriptures enfold us in the uplifted consciousness of the author.

The same thing happens when you place yourself in the presence of people who have the positive qualities that you yourself want to develop. You will not only gain intellectually from listening to their thoughts but you will become magnetically charged with some of the qualities of energy that have drawn success to them. Of course this is also true in reverse. If you spend time in the magnetism of negative people, you run the risk of taking on their qualites of negativity.

In order to use the mind to help us in our efforts to live in harmony with the positive flow we need to develop our powers of observation. Look consciously at life around you. Observe nature, people, current events, buildings, art and music; anything that comes across your path. Then mentally reach out to discern what qualities of consciousness are being expressed by that which you observe.

Try to mentally enter into the object of your observation. Don't just think about the object of your observation: try to mentally be it. In the stories about young King Arthur, Arthur's teacher Merlin had him focus on a fish in the moat until Arthur actually made the leap from looking at the fish to becoming the fish. We all think of this story as a fantasy. But it is an actual potential. I would not put trying to be a fish too high on a list of things to accomplish in this life, but the possibilities in life are so much greater than we are used to considering. We need to break free from the idea that anything is impossible.

This reaching out with your mind's eye will help you to lose identification with your smaller self and become more identified with your larger Self - all of life. It will also help you to actually perceive the magnetic vibrations, or qualities of consciousness, that we talked about in the last chapter. As you develop your ability to observe and inwardly feel the vibrational essence of things around you, you will begin to consciously perceive the energies in life that are uplifting and those that are downward-pulling.

Once we have opened this new gate of perception we need to apply discrimination to the process of observation. Keep in mind that discrimination is not judgment. It is not necessary to put others down in order to acknowledge that we do not want to be like them. We do not have to hate a lake for having water unfit to drink. We simply recognize the water as unhealthy and refrain from drinking it. This proper use of discrimination enables us to chart a safe and expanding course through life. If we do not use our discrimination we may end up being run down by a car because the crosswalk sign said stop before we were all the way across the street...so we stopped!

Way of the Positive Flow

The progressive use of our discriminative faculties is one of the ways that we can reach towards true wisdom. In India a follower of the path of discrimination looks for truth by examining all of life. The seeker says, "Not this, not this," when truth is not found. By eliminating everything that is not truth, the seeker eventually unveils that which is eternally true.

Service

Along with our efforts to reach out mentally and discriminate comes our need to act in life. This world we live in demands that we act. The blessing of this circumstance is that it keeps us moving. The ever-present issue is which way are we moving? Are we growing towards infinite freedom in Spirit or are we increasing our confinement to the limitations of the body and the ego?

How can we use attunement to the positive flow to choose actions that will lead to happiness?

Here is the basic precept: Decisions that expand our consciousness reflect the positive flow. Decisions that contract our consciousness represent the negative flow.

When we act with the right consciousness we cause the energy of our inner being to rise up the spine and to be focused at the point between the eyebrows - which is the seat of spiritual awareness in the body. This upward motion of energy in the physical and astral spines is the result of our connection to the positive flow. This positive flow of energy up the spine helps to release us from negatively binding energies of the past and allows our consciousness to expand.

When the energy in the body and mind are going down the spine towards the ego and selfishness, we are contracting ourselves and aligning our consciousness with the negative flow. This alignment can often be seen in the harsh expressions and cold uncaring eyes of those who choose to be hurtful instead of helpful toward others.

True inspirations from the positive flow will always bring about a positive potential for everyone affected by that inspiration. People may not choose to accept that positive potential, but it is always there if the positive flow is being expressed. Sometimes we are not sure if our ideas are true inspirations or a manifestation of our personal desires. When this happens, choices that are selfless and giving should be given greater credence.

Giving can be a mental, as well as, a physical act. We can give our time, wealth, ideas, physical energies, love, prayers, anything that is ours to give. The important thing to remember is that when we give with the right spirit we are aligning ourselves with the positive flow.

The goal is to always express the consciousness of selfless giving no matter what we are doing or how our efforts are received. Even if we are being paid to do a job it is important to have the consciousness that we are acting without the thought of what we are going to receive in return. When we live consistently with this attitude we will begin to see how the powers of the positive flow are supporting us in miraculous ways each and every day. This is how having the right attitude helps us to identify with ever-larger realities.

Even from a selfish point of view it makes sense to live in a way that keeps us connected to the largest realities possible. When we work only for our employer and they go out of business, we may get nothing. However, God will never go out of business, so if we work always for God our good efforts are money in the bank!

Another reason acting selflessly is so valuable is that when we forget ourselves by helping others we loosen the grip that our negative tendencies have on us. As we weaken the ego's tendency for self-involvement we will free ourselves from the bouts of negative feelings to which many people succumb.

I am not suggesting that we never give ourselves a break and explore personal areas of interest. Keeping our lives in balance through hobbies, recreation and time spent alone actually helps us to serve others more effectively. I am just pointing out that if we observe people who are consistently happy; they are invariably givers and not takers.

The amazing thing is that selflessness is really the ultimate positive form of selfishness because the more we give, the more we will automatically receive through the laws of magnetic attraction - and it helps others as well! This is another great thing about living in the positive flow; when we do it right, everyone wins! The positive flow short circuits the need for one person's gain to be at the cost of another person's loss.

Love

From a physical point of view, water and air would be considered the most essential ingredients for life. From a spiritual perspective love is the most essential ingredient. Ultimately all of life is an expression of the infinite ocean of Love. Love is the one thing that all people want. We are happiest when we feel love flowing through us. To the extent that we do not feel love, our darkest hour is at hand.

The lack of feeling loved is one of the strongest forces that keeps us looking outside of ourselves for happiness. And yet, it is that very search outside of ourselves that keeps us from perceiving love as the very substance from which we are made.

The universal love that is at the root of the positive flow is not the emotional passion that some people call love. Emotional passion is a dim reflection of true love. Understanding the difference between the emotions and soul perception is central to growing our ability to live connected to ever larger realities.

The emotions by their nature are temporary and subject to upheaval. They reflect the current status of the ego and often turn against the object of "love" like the black widow spider. When we live in our emotions we attach ourselves to our smaller self. This limits us and reflects a negative direction. When we root our love in soul awareness rather than ego awareness we begin to tap into our connection to the universal love of the positive flow.

Tuning in to the Positive Flow - Part 1

This is not to say that we want to excessively suppress our emotions and live in a world devoid of emotion - like Mr. Spock in Star Trek. What we want to do is increase our attunement to the positive flow so that instead of our feelings going out towards the emotions, they go in towards our connection to Spirit. By turning our attention within ourselves we will begin to refine our ability to feel ever greater levels of true selfless love. This is the kind of love that the saints express. It is the love that made and sustains the universe.

Meditation

Pulling together these three ways of aligning ourselves with the positive flow is the science and art of meditation. Meditation is the process of working consciously with our inner connection to the positive flow.

The predicament that we find ourselves in is that no matter how hard we work on discriminating, serving and loving, the tangled web of the mind keeps us from achieving complete success.

Why?

The main thrust of the negative flow is to convince us that happiness will be found outside of ourselves through the senses. As we have seen before the negative flow is the great deceiver. If we want to cultivate our direct connection with our source in the positive flow we must do it by turning our gaze within ourselves. This is what the saints and sages of all times and places have done.

When we meditate we are consciously calming the storm of agitation that our daily lives leave on the waters of the mind. Meditation techniques are designed specifically to calm the breath and thus the mind, so that we can feel who we are without all of the uproar that is caused by stimulation of the senses. Once the mind is calm it can be focused in order to penetrate the veil of illusion that separates us from the awareness of the love and joy that is our true nature. Calmness of mind leads to clear perception of the positive flow.

31

Way of the Positive Flow

To understand why meditation works we have to come back to the principles of magnetism. What we are trying to do is align all of the "molecules" of our consciousness so that they are working together as a team. The problem is that our long involvement in the ups and downs of life has kept our minds so stirred up we are not calm enough to see what is going on in there.

More than just bringing us to a calmer state of mind, deep meditation techniques begin to release the energies of the past that we have stored in our astral bodies. These energies cannot be uprooted through mental effort alone, even if we were willing and able to face them all. So much water has gone under the bridge of our experiences we need to deal with the whole of our consciousness rather than trying to deal with our past one experience at a time.

Through the regular practice of deep meditation we find that we are not improving just one part of our life but the whole of our life. Meditation will help all of the physical, mental/emotional, and spiritual areas of our being. Of course, it takes some time to become proficient at meditation. Therefore we work with improving the things that we can see now while we develop our ability to perceive ever larger parts of the whole picture.

When we consciously work on sharpening our discrimination, cultivating an attitude of selfless service and expanding our true loving nature we will find ourselves living with deeper and deeper attunement to the positive flow. It will become such a natural expression of who we are that we will wonder how we could have lived any other way.

Chapter 6
Tuning in to the
Positive Flow
Part 2

A calm mind and heart are the main prerequisites for being able to perceive the underlying energies behind our challenges in life. Calmness is also needed in order to access the solutions to those challenges. Throughout history the greatest exponents in all areas of endeavor almost always acknowledge that some higher power was the inspiration for their success. The ability to receive inspiration from that higher source requires inner calmness.

No matter what area of life we want to explore, the creative expression of our highest capabilities comes through our connection to the positive flow. When we put out a lot of energy towards anything in life we are creating a magnetic field that will eventually draw the result that we are seeking. The success of our efforts will depend on how much energy we can focus on our goal, our ability to keep these efforts going for as long as necessary and our openness to inspirations that will help us manifest the goal.

This is not about instantly materializing anything that we want, although that is certainly a potential. It is about reaching beyond the things that we think we want to the things that would be most beneficial for ourselves and for those around us. Often we do not know what we want in life; we just know that there is a need, a need for a feeling of fulfillment. As we practice living in the positive flow we will begin to get a clearer picture of that which is appropriate for our lives.

The overall raising of our energy and consciousness through the practice of the precepts that we have been discussing aligns our internal energies and gets them all working together harmoniously. When we start to feel this inner harmony permeating our lives, we will find that all of life around us responds to it. Not only will you be aware of it, but your family and friends will notice it as well. They may even ask you what has changed in your life. They may attribute your radiant face to your diet, new friends or anything else "outside" that could explain it. Only if they have begun to explore their own inner lives will they suspect that it is your inner consciousness that has changed.

Along with the overall uplifting of our consciousness we can use our connection with the positive flow to come up with solutions to any of the specific challenges that we face. In order to do this we need to learn how to use the broadcasting and receiving apparatus that we have within us.

To broadcast a need we focus our inner attention at the point between the eyebrows just above the nose. This point is also known as the spiritual eye. Learning to meditate will help us to develop our ability to do this because focusing on the spiritual eye is a basic part of meditation.

The frontal lobe of the brain is where we focus our attention anytime we are concentrating deeply on a subject. It is the seat of concentration in the body. You can even see people knit their eyebrows together when they are concentrating deeply. This outward tension is a muscular response to the inner focusing of the mind. Through the practice of meditation we learn to focus our attention at the point between the eyebrows with complete concentration, but without creating any physical tension.

In the beginning the best time to try broadcasting a need will be when you are sitting in the silence after practicing a meditation technique. Through regular practice this will become as natural to you as eating and sleeping. Once you get the knack of it, bring your awareness of this inner connection into your daily activities. The goal is to live life always connected to this inner line of communication.

The center in the body for receiving inner guidance and inspiration is the heart. This is where we are able to feel the rightness of any response that we might perceive in our mind. Why the heart? For each of us, the center of the universe is a point of intuitive perception in the heart center of our causal and astral bodies. The physical heart corresponds to this center. This is why we feel love in the heart. There certainly isn't anything about the pumping action of the physical heart that should inspire us to associate the heart with love. It is this center's subtle connection to universal love that animates our mental awareness that love is centered in the heart. Doesn't it make sense that the place we are most able to feel human love would be a connecting point to universal love?

In the beginning after you broadcast your need, your mind might begin to roam amongst different solutions that you may already have considered but are not sure which, if any, is the right solution. Keep your mind as calm as possible. When your mind is calm a new thought or a clearer version of one that you have already had will present itself to you. If you have received the answer clearly you will intuitively know that it is right. Your whole being will resonate with the rightness of it. If you are not sure, you can proceed by focusing most of your attention in the heart. As you then present each possibility to the spiritual eye, when you get to the right one you will feel an expanding sense of rightness about it in your heart.

Needless to say, this will take some practice, but not as much as you might think. This is not something that is available only to those who seclude themselves on a mountaintop. The portal to the positive flow is always open and available to those who make the right effort to be in tune with it. When you have advanced in your efforts you will find instant answers to the questions that need an immediate response.

There are two essential components to developing this inner connection with the positive flow. The first is the amount of positive energy that we put into our effort. If we just give it a few moments when we are in desperate need we cannot fairly expect much in the way of results. Many people pray only when they are in serious trouble. While this is better than never, it is what one might call being a bad weather friend and is not the best way to cultivate a relationship.

The truth is that God knows all of our thoughts: always. Our effort to attune ourselves to the positive flow is our part of the relationship. If we want to know our creator through direct perception of the positive flow we need to give it some serious effort.

The way that we focus our effort is through the use of will power. The will is the part of our consciousness that controls the volume of energy that we bring to bear on anything in life. The axiom is: The greater the will, the greater the flow of energy. It is through will power that our concentration is focused and given the forward moving momentum that brings results.

As an example, here is a true story that a good friend of mine told me.

There were two young men trying to carry a heavy refrigerator up some stairs without a dolly. These men were quite large. Their muscles bulged with their efforts and they enjoyed the sensation of that bulging because it made them feel strong. As they passed by a mirror they noticed with a smile how pleasantly large their muscles looked.

An old man came upon these two huffing and puffing he-men. Seeing that the young bucks were taking a long time to deal with the situation the old man told them, "That's not how you do it!" Before their astonished faces the old man picked up the refrigerator by himself and speedily carried it up the stairs; leaving the two "strong men" to wonder what had just happened.

This is just one of the ways that we can use will power. Will power can draw energy to our bodies or our minds. We use will power to connect to our inner source in meditation. Will power is the way that we marshal our inner energies in the direction that we want to go. Without will power we are like a boat with no sail or rudder, adrift with no way to harness the wind that is available to move us.

Keep in mind that will power is more about being willing to have ever greater amounts of energy and inspiration flowing through us, rather than grim, "I am the doer" determination. It is true that sometimes we need to dig in and "grin and bear" a situation. Not every task in life is easy, but when we are in tune with the positive flow we find that as our will power increases we also experience an increasingly cheerful sense of well-being. Laughter, a smile, a friendly word, a cheerful helping hand - these are all signs that our will power is attuned to the positive flow.

If you energetically apply yourself to cultivating the things we have been discussing you will find, even if your efforts seem to be getting nowhere, that one day you will look back at your life and see how it has wonderfully changed. You will find that you were so busy doing good that you hadn't noticed that you yourself had become good.

In order to anticipate success we need to look into every aspect of life and consciously choose how we want to live it. We need to say "yes" to all of the positive influences that we can place around us, because this task of self-realization is not easy. We all need as much help as we can get. Surrounding ourselves with positively charged influences will strengthen and magnetize our efforts, increasing our chances of success.

The second important aspect to our efforts is the avoidance, as much as possible, of those things that impede our progress. Remember, this is not about judging what others do or do not do. It is about consciously choosing the way you want to live. If you are presented a piece of rotten food you will choose not to eat it. You know that it will be bad for your health. It is the same with all areas of life: job, family, church, recreation, health care and community. It is wise to avoid people, places and situations that you are not yet able to handle without being negatively affected by them.

Many people buy into the ways of the world thinking, "Well, there isn't anything that I can do about it." While it is true that most of us are not going to be able to completely insulate ourselves from the negative influences of society as a whole there is still much that we can do to help ourselves if we choose to. We will be discussing some of these ways in coming chapters. As you practice living in tune with the positive flow you will find that you are able to come up with the ways that work for you - in your situation. That is what this is all about! Each of us will apply these principles in our own unique combination. While you experiment with these ideas remember to always refer back to the basic underlying principles that unite us all. While we want to be creative we do not want to wander off on our own and get lost.

Some people become concerned about being too different or separate from the mainstream of society. They think that it is unhealthy to stand outside of the group. Well, look at mainstream society. Is that what you want for your life? If so, then go ahead. But if you want to change yourself you will need to support those changes as much as possible until they become strong enough to stand on their own no matter what the circumstances in which you find yourself.

If you were learning to play a musical instrument and you put so much time into it that your friends did not see you very much, they might think you were being a little fanatical about it, but they would not give it too much thought. It is different when you try to change yourself spiritually. If you really apply yourself to the task invariably someone you know will complain that you are becoming a fanatic. That person may also feel compelled to inform you that you are going about it the wrong way. They might even ask you to consider trying their religious affiliation. This is one of the ways that people are unknowingly used by the negative flow to impede the progress of those who have begun making a conscious effort to attune their lives to the positive flow.

In fact, in the beginning of your efforts it is often better that you do not tell anyone. Just do it as an experiment in living. Test these ideas out for yourself. If you find your life improving, then keep it up. If you do not find any results, then be sure you are practicing this approach properly. If after that you are not getting the results that you want, chuck it! In any case, do not let disbelievers keep you from exploring life for yourself.

Throughout the 1960's many people were still saying that mankind would never walk on the moon. Even after man had landed on the moon some people said it was all a hoax and that they did not believe any of it; that it had been staged. History shows us that there are always people, even amidst overwhelming evidence to the contrary, who simply refuse to believe that which is true.

Living in tune with the positive flow is an instance where you can "go to the moon" yourself. You can experience the validity of these truths in the laboratory of your own life. All you have to do is start consciously experimenting instead of letting the laboratory run itself.

Chapter 7
Way of the Positive Flow

The *Way of the Positive Flow* is an overall approach to how we live our lives. It is also the application of the principles that we have been discussing toward a specific technique. This technique can be used at all times in all situations. This is the way we bring all of our understanding into the moment by moment challenges of our lives.

The *Way of the Positive Flow* can be defined as: the continuous process of perception, attunement and experimentation - through the positive redirection of energy - as applied to living in the positive flow of life.

Let's look at the individual components of this technique and then put them all together.

Perception

Perception is the power of observation that we discussed earlier. It is the conscious reaching out with our inner awareness in order to perceive the underlying energies of life around us. It requires a calm sense of focus, a non-judgmental attitude and an open heart. The more that we are aware of life around us as being our own larger Self, the more capable we will become with our powers of perception.

Remember, this is not in its essence something that we do through the senses. Yes, we use our senses to bring in information about what is going on around us. But more

40

importantly, we need to feel the energies underneath that which we see, hear, touch, smell and taste.

When our awareness is in our physical senses as we first walk into a room we are aware of the sounds, the lighting, the way people are dressed and maybe the decor of the room. We may hear laughter or meet silence. We may look at the faces of the people in the room or notice what people are doing. We might smell the odor of food in the air. All of the input that we receive from our outward observations will give us a surface impression of what is going on in the room.

Our inner perception can give us a picture of the energies that lay underneath all of those outward signals. This inner perception may confirm what our senses tell us or it may open up to us a completely different picture. What we are looking for with our inner awareness is the qualities of energy underneath the picture that our senses paint. We are trying to perceive the group energy, the qualities of magnetism that create the vibrational "feel" of our surroundings.

In the 1960's the terms "good vibes" and "bad vibes" became part of the public nomenclature. There was even a hit song by the Beach Boys called *Good Vibrations*. In the 1970's the Star Wars movies brought the concept of a universal consciousness called, The Force. The main character Luke Skywalker was exhorted by his teacher Obi-Wan Kenobi to inwardly reach out and feel: The Force.

The idea that we can feel vibrations of consciousness around us and receive information and inspiration from these perceptions is not new. It is just new to us in our personal attempts to explore what is real in our lives versus that which is fantasy in books, movies and music. The scientific approach to this possibility is to experiment and see for ourselves if it is true.

In the beginning it will be difficult to tune out sensory input while you tune in to the more subtle energies. The more you focus your inner attention at the spiritual eye the less you will be distracted by your senses.

Way of the Positive Flow

When your senses receive laughter you might think that the people in the room are happy. Then, when you look out with your inner perception, you may find confirmation in a feeling that the energies expressed are those of good natured joy. On the other hand, your inner perception may tell you that the laughter is a whipping up of emotional energies in order to crowd out boredom rather than the experience of real joy.

It is essential that this not be a process of judging others. It is simply the opening up of a deeper way of perceiving what is going on in life. Inner perception is a powerful tool. Like any other tool it can be used to help or to harm. If our perceptions separate us from others by increasing our ego awareness, it will be harming us. If it helps us to expand our sympathies and improve ourselves it is a blessing. Only with careful attention to our own energies can we maintain the right attitude towards life as it unfolds before us.

With practice you can live with your inner perception always comfortably in the forefront of your consciousness. This way you will not often be fooled by what the senses tell you. When someone smiles at you, you will be able to feel the energy underneath that smile. When someone offers to do you a favor, you will sense the spirit in which the offer is made. If you are looking at a new home or apartment you will be able to recognize the qualities of the building and the vibrations of the surrounding area.

One thing that you want to be careful not to do is color the energies that you perceive with your own desires or preferences. The mind most often sees what it wants or expects to see. That is why a calm and impersonal mind is essential to the real use of inner perception.

The axiom is: Reason follows feeling.

As a result, how you personally feel about something causes your reason to come up with a rationale to support those feelings. When you observe life from a perspective that is detached from your own personal likes and dislikes, you can begin to see things for what they really are. How you personally feel about what you perceive and what you do about those feelings are separate issues.

You may be saying to yourself that you have already experienced this type of awareness. This is not surprising since it is the most natural thing in the world to do. The really amazing thing is that so many people turn off this natural way of opening themselves up to life in favor of the much more limiting view of the senses and ego alone.

Make it a practice to live more and more from this inner perspective. Use it to understand deeper and deeper levels of every area of your life. This ability to reach out and see what is going on underneath the surface of life will not only help you to see and deal with that which is right in front of you, but it will help you to anticipate things that have not yet arrived. The power of inner observation is an essential tool if you truly want to know what is going on within yourself and in life all around you. Once you discover how to live with this inner view, your life will never be the same.

Attunement

The attunement part of our formula has to do with tuning in to the positive flow for the solutions to whatever your situation may be. It is basically the same as perception except you are focusing your inner awareness on solutions from within rather than trying to perceive the energies around you.

Once you have observed something in life you arrive at the question we discussed in the first chapter: So, what do I do now? Well, here is the answer. Once you have perceived the energies of any situation in life you attune yourself to the positive flow of universal understanding in order to receive ideas about how to proceed.

The positive flow is the storehouse of all knowledge: past, present and future. In eternity, time as we perceive it does not exist. When we attune ourselves to the inner wisdom of the positive flow we will magnetically draw to our lives the highest expression of truth that we are capable of understanding at the time.

One of the things that keep people from being able to tune into the positive flow is the idea that there is only one right answer for any given situation. In the West we seek to find a single definitive solution for every question or situation. We want to find one answer - that is the best answer. In the East there is a tradition of seeing many valid interpretations for understanding any particular issue or situation. As we approach the potential solutions for any challenge that we might face in our lives, remember that truth is flexible. It flows with the ever changing energies of the creation. So there may be many workable solutions to any given situation. The thing we want to do is attune ourselves to the subject as a whole and then open ourselves up to the possibilities that present themselves.

The positive flow is the source of all creativity, so expect the unexpected. Be open to new and unforeseen ways of expressing positive energies through your life. When you paint a painting there are an infinite number of ways the picture can be made. Often when you start a creative project you begin with one expectation and end up with a totally different result.

Flowing with the creative potential of life is part of the fun! At the same time, if you flow all over the place, you may find that all you have is one big mess! What we need to do is balance our creativity with the focus that is necessary for the completion of any given task. If you fix your goal in your mind as you are attuning to the positive flow you will find very specific ideas available to you. If you let your mind float generally around the subject you may receive a wide range of possibilities.

Gradually, as you become more experienced in working with the positive flow you will get a feel for what works in general, as well as what is right for any given situation in particular. It is this very real, personal relationship with the positive flow that you want to explore and develop.

Way of the Positive Flow

Most people do not experience their attunement with the positive flow as a voice, pronouncing the will of God! What happens is that along with generating their own common sense solutions they open themselves up to higher inspiration. Sometimes they receive something that they can cognize and sometimes they do not. What is interesting is that most of the time it doesn't matter whether one consciously receives anything or not. The most common result for people who try to live in harmony with the positive flow is that they simply do just that. They experience an overall harmony in their lives in such a way that the desperate materialization of a new idea is rarely needed.

The potential for accessing and utilizing the positive flow is as individual as each one of us. The key for each of us is to consciously tap that potential to the best of our ability. Our attempts to do so will not only improve the specifics of our lives, but they will hasten the longer rhythms of our lives that are bringing us ever closer to our home in Spirit.

Experiment/Redirect

Because life is a flow we cannot assume that the inspirations of today are the appropriate ones for tomorrow. In fact, that which is in the flow for this instant could be flowing the wrong way in the next. Fortunately, the directions that we are supposed to go don't often leave us looking quickly from side to side like spectators at a ping pong match. The thing to keep in mind is that as we move forward we are experimenting with that which we currently perceive as the correct action. The more experience we gain working with the flow the better we will be at following with determination and flexibility, simultaneously.

Through your practice you will gain confidence in the inspirations that guide you. At the same time, you also need to be willing to be wrong. At any time you must be willing to say, "This doesn't feel right." Or, "I think I've made a mistake." If you become attached to thinking you are right and start to think, "I have the power of the positive flow behind me, so nobody

45

better get in my way!", you will definitely not be radiating the qualities of energy that are indicative of attunement to the positive flow. So, be willing to change course at any time.

There is a tendency for some to think that any kind of resistance to a perceived inspiration is a sign to change direction. That is not the case. Life is given to us as a challenge to improve ourselves. These challenges wouldn't be challenges if they were all easy. So difficulty in itself should not be seen as a sign of misdirection.

The best sign of misdirection is an uneasy feeling in the heart. When you feel that: pay attention. The heart is our compass. Once we learn to feel its calmness, we will be able to recognize when that calmness is disturbed. This is another important reason for meditation. Not only does meditation calm the physical heart, it vibrationally calms the energy of our heart center. Through meditation we release the agitation that fogs our inner vision.

While we are experimenting with ways to implement our inspirations we need to work with the energies at hand in a way that doesn't disconnect us from the positive flow. Sometimes people get so excited from their inspirations they just take off at full speed until they get who knows where and then wonder, "What happened?" Other times we find that while our energies are in sync with the flow, people that we are working with just can't seem to flow in the same direction.

Blending our own energies with the energies of others in positive ways is one of the great keys to success. It is much easier to work with, rather than against, ourselves and others. This is where the concept of redirecting the energy comes in.

The next time you find yourself working with people who are not getting along or when your own mental citizens start to rebel, rather than standing up in front and commanding everyone to, "Do what I say!", see if you can apply some energy in just the right place in order to get things moving back on track.

Way of the Positive Flow

This is an idea that is well known in the martial arts. If someone throws a punch at you, rather than standing firm and taking it head on you just side step it. Instead of trying to stop it you let it move past you. As it goes past just a little twist of the attacker's wrist can send them tumbling off in a direction away from you. The attacker's forward momentum is used to achieve your goal of protecting yourself. This redirection of their energy, from hitting you to moving them off in another direction, is much easier than trying to stop it directly.

It is the same when you work with all types of energy. Rather than going directly against the current direction of momentum, try to redirect it by sensitively applying energy in order to redirect the situation into the way that you think is best. This works with yourself, other individuals (including kids!), groups, animals, plants, in fact with all life.

Here is another example.

Let's say someone is yelling at you. It doesn't really matter who or why. If you try to go against them they will probably dig in their heels in support of their feelings. If you start yelling back, you won't feel peaceful in yourself and you probably won't stop them from yelling. The situation might even get worse. Depending on who is yelling at you and why, there are various things you can do.

Remember, you have to take into account who they are and who you are. If you stay calm something will occur to you. What you want to do is get their mind off of the yelling track, so you have to introduce the need for new thinking on their part. One simple thing to do is ask, "Can I get you a glass of water?" or "If they are crying, here let me get you a tissue."

Asking almost any question off the subject they are yelling about will often cause them to pause and think. As soon as they do that you have your chance to take things to the next level by saying, "You know, I agree with you, and I would really like to help you." or "I am so sorry this has happened, let me see what I can do to help you."

Way of the Positive Flow

If you can't come up with a question or your questions don't work, then you might consider simply walking away - like my mother did when I had a tantrum in the store. You can say as you walk away, "I will be back when you have calmed down."

There is also the no reaction approach, just stay calm in yourself and wait for the storm to pass. When they see they aren't going to get anything done by yelling, they will eventually stop.

In any case, don't let other people's emotions determine your level of happiness. When we live inwardly connected to the positive flow we will feel well protected when facing even in the largest emotional storm.

Of course there are times when it is necessary to stand firm in life and insist that others behave. When that happens, keep in mind that what we are trying to do is short circuit the negative energies being expressed. Once those negative energies have dissipated, begin to work the formula again. Experiment with redirecting things in a positive direction.

Negative energies will try to cling wherever they can, so when a negative situation is resolved be sure that you inwardly let go of any negativity that may have penetrated into your consciousness. Resentment and other negative feelings will draw you into your own personal storm of negativity. Practice non-attachment, forgiveness and humility as you work this formula.

This process of experimentation/redirection of energy should always be attuned to the positive flow. Perception/observation and inner attunement to the flow are the grease that keeps the wheels of our experiments in life from overheating. When you apply this formula to all of your life you will find broad new vistas of potential opening up. The foremost will be an ever-greater feeling of harmony within yourself, the world around you and with your creator.

Chapter 8
Five Natural Expressions of the Positive Flow

Here are five ways that the positive flow will naturally express itself through us when we have perfected our attunement. They are: non-violence, non-lying, non-stealing, non-sensuality and non-covetousness. By consciously cultivating these qualities in our lives we will hasten our ability to harmonize with the positive flow. Intellectual understanding of these ideas is just the first step. Once we grasp the essence of these principles we need to apply them in practical ways on a daily basis. The goal is to spontaneously express these qualities as naturally as the way we breathe. When they are the norm in our lives we will know in body, mind and spirit that we are successfully living in the positive flow.

These five expressions are described using the prefix "non" to indicate that the root word is foreign to our nature. All of life is based on duality. So there are things in life that we should do and things that we should avoid. These qualities of consciousness cover areas that will naturally be avoided if we are living in harmony with the positive flow.

Non-Violence
Injury to oneself and others can take the form of physical, mental/emotional or spiritual harm. When we express energies whose purpose is to diminish others in any way we are acting with a consciousness of violence. There is a saying

that goes, "Small-minded people cut others down to make themselves appear bigger." This applies not only to people, but to all of life.

Unfortunately, no matter how hard we try, "stuff happens". People and other forms of life get hurt and even die as a result of our actions. The fact is that it is simply not physically possible for us to go through life without killing things. We kill bacteria in our bodies. We kill bugs as we walk down the street or drive our cars. Sometimes we need to kill domestic or wild animals for public safety or to end an animal's suffering. Police and soldiers are forced to kill others in the line of duty. Doctors are sometimes forced to choose between saving the life of a mother or her child.

Death is a part of life. So it cannot of itself be seen as out of harmony with life's plan. The key to understanding this has to do with the realities of our consciousness. All actions in life are precipitated by a quality or mixture of qualities of consciousness. If we harbor a desire to harm anyone or anything in life that desire alone is an expression of violence. These root desires eventually manifest themselves in our lives as our thoughts and actions.

When we have cleansed our inner selves of these negative energies, we will find our outward expression of life a beautiful flow of kinship with all life. The harmony that we feel inside ourselves will magnetize life around us into expressing that harmony as well. This is why even people with strong animosities towards each other find their negative energies diminished or even gone in the presence of a saint.

It doesn't take a saint to recognize that we should try to avoid hurting others. When we intentionally hurt others we strengthen the consciousness of being separate from others and all of life. This makes the wave of the ego stronger and keeps us from experiencing the ocean of infinite love and joy.

The real challenge that we face on a daily basis is not about killing but about just basically being nice to one another

Five Natural Expressions of the Positive Flow

in all circumstances, even if we don't feel like it. Learning proper behavior in trying circumstances is only the first step in attunement to the positive flow. As you experience energies from within yourself or moving towards you from others that make you want to strike out with hurtful thoughts or deeds practice redirecting those energies through the use of our formula.

One of the most basic tenets of life in the positive flow is that we are all one. If we hurt others, we are only hurting our own larger Self. We are also activating the law of cause and effect in such a way as to bring that same quality of energy back to us at some time in the future. This principle turned to our benefit means that when we have truly cultivated the consciousness of non-violence, the negative flow will lose its power to do violence to us.

Non-Lying

Most children are taught that telling a lie is bad, but few are taught the real reasons why. The importance of truthfulness goes far beyond the moral strictures of the "golden rule". After all, what is truth? It is usually defined as that which is factually correct, but truth is much deeper than that. Remember, life is a flow - so is truth.

Consider these examples:

Johnny threw a ball through a window. That is a fact, but the truth could be that he did it on purpose or the truth could be that he did it by accident.

Sally is now dating her best friend's old boyfriend. Did she steal him away? Or did things just happen without her conscious volition?

These first two examples are fairly straightforward, but what about this next example?

Mike, Bob and Mitch, three teenagers, were all looking at a motorcycle parked on the street. Mitch accidentally knocked it over. Just then the bigger than life owner of the motorcycle came outside and asked, "Who knocked down my motorcycle?" Mike stepped forward and answered, "I did."

Way of the Positive Flow

Is there any way that Mike could be telling the truth?

In India there is a scriptural saying that states: A lower truth ceases to be truth in the light of a higher truth. Through this axiom we can see that truth is relative to the highest truth that can be expressed at the time, so the highest truth isn't necessarily the same as the factual truth. In this case, Mike felt that he was more able to handle the situation than Mitch. Mike nobly offered himself as a shield. This selflessness made his truth higher than the fact that Mitch had actually committed the offense.

Mike's solution would have been even better if he had stepped forward and said truthfully that it was an accident. This would have expressed the factual truth and deflected the energy away from Mitch.

Let me make it clear that I am not suggesting we make up clever rationalizations for thinking or acting improperly. Truth is not whatever we can intellectually justify. Here is the principle: Truth lives at the heart of all things and not at their perimeter. Truth is most centrally connected to the positive flow and takes into consideration all of the different energies that make up the totality of a situation. Under complex circumstances those who are truly wise are needed to plumb the depths of a situation. The underlying truths behind all experiences can be found in the positive flow, but it takes a truthful person to find them!

It is only through increasing the magnetism of our inner and outer truth that we can build the power to draw ever higher levels of truth into our lives. The building of this magnetism starts with always speaking the factual truth. Only once we are firmly established on that level of honesty can we graduate to higher levels of truth and understanding. Those who try to jump to the head of the class without working their way up through the ranks often find themselves in over their heads.

Earlier in our discussion we talked about self-honesty and how it is essential as a foundation for our inner health. It is

Five Natural Expressions of the Positive Flow

not enough to be truthful to others; we also need to be truthful to ourselves. The combined magnetism of our inner honesty and our truthful words is what allows the power of the universe to stand behind us. Each time we speak the truth, inwardly and outwardly, we are adding energy to the magnetism of our word. Each time we are false, we diminish that power. Through truthfulness we build a strength that will support our efforts in every aspect of our lives.

Non-Stealing

Not taking what belongs to another is a fairly straight-forward precept. It doesn't take much explanation for even a young child to understand the injustice that occurs when something is stolen. As a practical matter, stealing only sets us up for a negative experience in our future. If we take things that are not ours the universe will respond by relieving us of that which is ours at some time in the future. The law of cause and effect is quite exacting.

Many people do not give enough attention to the reason why someone is tempted to steal and how that causative energy can keep us from happiness, even if we do not actually steal anything.

The motivating expression of consciousness behind stealing is desire. Desire for that which isn't ours is one of the greatest powers that the negative flow has to hinder our happiness. It is interesting, and typical of how the negative flow tricks us, to note that we are led to believe that the more we have of "things" the happier we will be. So we desire more, which causes us to be sad - since we don't have that which we desire. If our desires lead us to cross the line of propriety and we steal that which we want, greater suffering can be the only result.

The simple, yet somehow hidden truth is that if we look closely at the lives of those who have "everything" they are not more but less inclined to be happy. When a person thinks that the fulfillment of their desires will make them happy and they fulfill those desires, yet they aren't happy, where do they go from there? Unfortunately despair, drugs and alcohol are the most common refuge for those that feel the anguish of either unfulfilled desires or the backlash of realizing that lasting happiness cannot be found through material possessions, the senses or the emotions.

As long as we desire things that we do not have we put a limit on our ability to feel the all-succoring joy of the positive flow. The axiom concerning desires is: What comes of itself let it come. If life presents us with sweets; fine. If life serves us bitter herbs; fine. As long as we keep our attention on the inner satisfaction of the positive flow, pleasant and unpleasant fluctuations of life will not be able to steal away our happiness. This does not mean that we should not try to improve things when life goes against our preferences. It means that we should rise above outward ups and downs by maintaining our inner connection to the joy of the positive flow.

Non-Sensuality

We have already talked about how immersion in the senses leads to desires, which leads to a lack of ability to feel the inner peace of our home in Spirit. This is one of the main reasons why we want to avoid over-involvement with the senses.

Keep in mind that it is not that the senses are "bad". It is an issue of what we want to do with the energy that flows into our consciousness through the senses. If that input limits our awareness of our higher nature then we can choose to take control of the situation by limiting the volume of sensual input. We can also learn to translate, or transmute, our experience of sense stimulations into greater inner awareness rather than limited outer awareness.

The way that we keep our awareness from going out towards the senses when they are stimulated is to turn our attention inward towards the seat of spiritual awareness at the point between the eyebrows. As the energy moves from the source of stimulation towards the brain we want to use this

Five Natural Expressions of the Positive Flow

energy to increase our inner connection to Spirit rather than letting it take us towards outward sense awareness. By focusing our attention on the spiritual eye during sensory stimulation we are engaging in the process of redirecting the energy towards the positive flow rather than letting it take us outward towards the negative flow. This holds true for everything from feeling a cool breeze on the forehead to sexual orgasm. As we develop this ability to use outward experiences to increase our inner connection to Spirit we will find that instead of being bound by the senses we can enjoy life fully with an inner sense of freedom.

Interestingly, this process is also a way to deal with physical pain. At a certain point the brain automatically withdraws the consciousness from intense pain. We can do this consciously by going into a higher, superconscious state rather than a lower subconscious state. The next time you feel pain do not define the sensation as pain. Let it be a sensation without a positive or negative label. Then redirect your awareness of the sensation into the spine and up to the spiritual eye. From that point visualize the energy dispersing into space.

The ability to redirect and ultimately withdraw our consciousness from the senses is key to our success in being aware of our inner Self and our relationship to the universe. If we can't calm our minds and bodies we simply will not be able to access the inner apparatus for perceiving Spirit. The more we live in the senses, the more we live on the periphery of our consciousness.

The senses are like spoiled children - they want, want, want. If we don't give them what they want, they have a tantrum and we end up in a bad mood. Then when we do indulge them, they never want to stop. So we overindulge them. Even if we don't make ourselves sick from overindulgence, we feel a natural let down after all that stimulation and so once again we are in a depressed mood. Moods are one of the most common results of over-stimulation of the senses.

Way of the Positive Flow

When it comes to the senses: The senses ever fed are never satisfied and the senses never fed are ever satisfied. Think about it.

Non-covetousness

Earlier we talked about not desiring that which belongs to another. Non-covetousness is about not desiring or being attached to that which is rightfully ours. A story will illustrate:

In the early 1900's there was a young man in India. His father was an executive for a railroad company so the family was well off by local standards.

After some cajoling the young man convinced his father to buy him a new motorcycle with a sidecar. This was a fairly extravagant item at the time but the father was generous and made the gift to his son. Soon the young man could be seen riding through town with his long hair streaming in the wind. Besides the convenience of having his own transportation it was great fun! Some months after getting the motorcycle an acquaintance of this young man stopped by and admired it with longing.

"You like it?" asked the young man of his acquaintance.

"Oh, yes!" responded the acquaintance. "But I could never afford to get one," he continued with a note of disappointment in his voice.

"Wait right here," said the young man as he turned and entered the house.

A few minutes later the young man came out of the house and handed his acquaintance the ownership papers to the motorcycle. "Here, it is yours," announced the young man. And so the motorcycle had a new owner.

When we can feel that free of all our possessions, we will be unencumbered by them. At the same time, freedom from attachment to our possessions is not the same as lack of appreciation. When the universe blesses us with bounty we should enjoy and care for that bounty. If the universe then takes that bounty away or inspires us to pass it on, we should accept

Five Natural Expressions of the Positive Flow

with appreciation that it was with us for a time and has now moved on to bless another.

All too often we do not realize what a burden possession can be. When we own a nice car we worry about it being dented or stolen. If we have a nice house with many fine things in it we worry about burglars or a fire. Even things that we do not really possess, but think of as our own, cause us worry. People with fame worry about keeping it. People in politics worry about being re-elected. Parents worry if their children really love them enough or if they might be injured. It goes on and on.

This can also apply to gifts that we receive from others. Often there is a sense of obligation that comes with the reception of a gift. If we bind ourselves to others because of what they give us we are, in a way, becoming their slaves. A true gift is given without any sense of obligation. It should also be received without any sense of obligation or attachment. If you ever feel that you are being given something that has strings attached, do your best to avoid receiving the gift. Try to redirect the energies of the situation so that you remain free of obligation.

The key is to remember that true happiness comes from within us. It is not dependent on any outward situation to be present in our lives. When we attach our happiness to things or circumstances outside of ourselves we are asking for trouble. Enjoy that which you have, while you have it, but don't let it own you because, "Chains though of gold still bind."

These five natural expressions of the positive flow - non-violence, non-lying, non-stealing, non-sensuality and non-covetousness - are states of consciousness to be attained and guidelines for achieving that attainment. Take the time to introspect on these energies in your own life. Apply our formula to making the kind of improvements that will bring you lasting happiness. If you accept the temporary ups and downs of life as all that you can hope for, that is where you will stay. Reach for the stars and you will find yourself rising to heights of consciousness that you never before imagined.

Chapter 9
Five Virtues of the Positive Flow

Just like the five natural expressions in the last chapter, when we find these five virtues flowing through our consciousness we will know that our efforts to attune our lives to the positive flow are working. They are: cleanliness, contentment, self-control, self-study and devotion to God.

Cleanliness

We all know the physical reasons why cleanliness is beneficial to the body. When we let our bodies and the physical environment become dirty, we open ourselves up to the greater possibility of disease. Since a lack of cleanliness would be considered a downward-pulling energy we can see how the energies of disease would be attracted to it. It is the same with our inner home. If we keep it clean the dirt of negative thoughts will not be able to enter and cause the disease of unhappiness.

One way to keep your inner house clean is to avoid that which will clutter the place up. Anything in life that lowers the vibration with which your soul resonates is for you dirty. All thoughts that are associated with downward-pulling energies leave the smudge of their presence when they pass through your consciousness. You wouldn't let someone with muddy boots track through the white pile carpet in your living room. So don't let people or places with negative vibrations enter into your mind or heart.

Five Virtues of the Positive Flow

Cleanliness of the mind and heart is not maintained by simply avoiding outward influences that may lower our vibration. Even if we could avoid all future negative influences, we all carry countless commitments of energy to negativity of the past. How do we get rid of all that stuff? We faithfully use the tools of discrimination, service, love and meditation. Along with helping us to avoid future negative energies these practices hasten our release from past escapades.

While love is in itself the most powerful force in the universe, without the experience of deep meditation it is very difficult to harness that power. The higher techniques of meditation are the fastest way to cleanse our consciousness from the past and strengthen it for the future. When we put love and meditation together we have an unbeatable combination.

All of the commitments of energy that we have stored in our astral bodies - the muddy boot prints of our past - will need to be expressed outwardly unless we can give the whole place a good vacuuming. The higher techniques of meditation work directly with the energy centers in the astral body where these commitments of energy have been swept under the rug. By using meditation techniques to consciously move the energy in the   astral body we can deeply clean our inner house.

When we utilize the positively magnetizing power of love and the cleansing power of meditation we will find our inner home shining with a purity that will move us gradually to that ultimate level of cleanliness: holiness.

Contentment

Contentment is said to be the supreme virtue. After all, isn't that how we would feel all of the time if we were one-hundred percent in tune with the positive flow? Why wait? Why not attune ourselves to the consciousness of contentment now? There is no time like the present to get our feet wet!

Too often in life we think in terms of "someday". Let today be that day. Let's take the ideal of contentment and start wearing it like we would any new set of clothes. At first it may feel a little stiff or we may even get stuck by a pin that didn't get thrown out with the wrapping. We will have to make some adjustments to how we react to life around us. So what? How much energy have we put into looking good on the outside? Let's direct some of that energy to being content on the inside.

Let's accept what our life is like today and connect ourselves to the inner happiness that is always available to us. If we let the circumstances of our lives dictate our level of happiness the best we can hope for is an up and down ride. Why not get off the roller coaster and live in peace?

This doesn't mean that we do not work to improve our outward circumstances when they could be better. It means that we should not let the ups and downs of everyday life keep us from being generally happy. Ultimately, we become so connected to the inner sanctum of the positive flow that no matter how rough the waters of our lives get, we still feel that inner peace.

Contentment is not a negative state of indifference to life. It is a dynamic state of consciousness that comes directly from the positive flow. Through consistent inner attunement to the positive flow you can live every day, regardless of the outward circumstances, in a vibration of positive acceptance and peaceful well-being. When your consciousness is flowing with contentment it will radiate out through your eyes like a warm fire on a cold night. When you feel real contentment you will not have to wonder, "When will I be happy?" You will be too busy being happy.

Self-control

In our quest to improve our lives self-control is essential. If we cannot marshal our energies in the directions of our goals what hope can we have of success in anything? We have all been given the powers of the universe to do with as we wish, so why don't we utilize them? Lack of self-control.

On the surface, self-control is making a choice and following through with that choice. Underneath the surface we can find the motivating energies that cause us to make any given choice in the first place. The guiding force in the choices of most people is desire, which is held captive by habit. As a result, habit becomes the gatekeeper of our desires. Once we have built an area of interest habit stands ready to remind us of the past and guide our future.

Most of us think that we are free in our choices in life. We think that we can go anywhere or do anything according to our whims, but those desires are only idle dreams unless we have the power - self-control - to manifest them.

Why is it that millions of dollars are spent each year on diet aids when we all know that the basic need for most people is to simply eat less and exercise more? Why do we go to the gym to exercise instead of exercising on our own at home? Why do we put off cleaning the garage? Or mowing the lawn? Why haven't we written that great American novel that we always wanted to write? Where did all the dreams go that we had when we were children?

The most consistent reason that we do not fulfill our goals in life is because of a lack of self-control. Once our energy gets going in any one direction we create a groove in our consciousness. That groove is called a habit. The more energy we put into that groove the deeper and more established it becomes. Once a habit becomes deep seated it takes a large amount of energy to change it. Of course good habits do not need changing, just continued support. But bad habits - energy patterns that hinder our positive progress in life - need to be addressed with a view to making the kinds of changes that will improve our lives.

Dealing with negative habits is one of the most fruitful areas in which to apply the principles of our formula. Some negative patterns are not all that difficult to deal with. If a person was raised without the regular brushing of their teeth, getting on track with brushing regularly should not be a major crisis in their life. The dentist bills might be! But the act of regular brushing can be established in a relatively short period of time with minimal effort.

So what do we do about areas of our life that are a big challenge?

When you decide to change your life don't leap off a cliff and try to transform everything on day one. While enthusiasm is an elevating quality, lack of practicality is downward-pulling. In the beginning choose something that you are fairly confident you can handle. With success in your first endeavor you will build momentum towards handling a larger task on your next effort. Build yourself up so that you develop your ability to apply our formula and strengthen your will power at the same time.

Remember the principles of our formula. Perceive the habit or direction of energy that you want to deal with. Attune yourself to creative ways of handling the situation. Then experiment with redirecting your energies in a positive direction.

Even more important than dealing directly with our negative habits is the efforts that we put into our positive habits. The more we increase the good things that we are doing in life the greater will be our positive magnetism. This positive magnetism will start to suck power away from the negative habits. Look for ways to do good things in your life. The more time you spend in positively charged endeavors the less you will be affected by negative energies of the past.

When we have freed ourselves from the energies of our negative habits and firmly established ourselves in the ways of the positive flow, we will truly be free.

Self-Study

Along with studying all of the great expressions of the positive flow that have come before us - no matter which part of life those works express - comes our need to study the part of life that is most central to each of us as an individual: our own Self. It is not enough to be well read and knowledgeable about many areas of life. Or even to be able to come up with the appropriate scriptural quote for all occasions. We need to understand who we are now so that we can become who we want to be.

The negative flow teaches us to view ourselves on the outside. Notice how concerned people are with how they look on the outside. They think, "If I look good, I am good." I'm not suggesting that we throw good personal grooming out the window altogether. However, this preoccupation with how our bodies look keeps many from finding the greatest beauty in life: that which is within us.

It is more productive to redirect that attention from viewing the outer body to paying close attention to our inner home. Keeping the contents of the mind in order is essential to moving forward. As we consciously seek to transform ourselves through attunement to the positive flow, the negative flow will endeavor to intervene in the situation. Only through regular introspection will we be able to keep an eye on things so that the cobwebs of negative energies can't spread unnoticed within us.

Even more important than our mental efforts to improve ourselves is the discovery of our larger Self that is always connected to our source in Spirit. As we learn to discriminate between that which is temporary and that which is permanent we will start to discover ourselves for the beautiful expressions of Spirit that we truly are. The more we know ourselves as manifestations of Spirit the more effective we will become at manifesting that which expresses God's view of our lives.

Devotion to God

While we discuss devotion to God, keep in mind that the word God means different things to different people. Many people think that because they believe in something intensely that in itself makes it true. When I refer to God I am talking about the reality of life beyond human opinion: that which is true regardless of what we call it or how we feel about it.

Way of the Positive Flow

Much of the value that can be obtained by practicing the things that we have been talking about can be received without a belief in God. The mechanics of how life works are not dependent upon our beliefs. Electricity can electrocute us whether we believe in it or not. We can express positive or negative qualities regardless of our views on the source of all life. Just keep in mind: if God exists, God exists whether we believe in God or not.

So why bother to believe in God?

If you go to the seashore you will see a large body of water. Your senses are not able to tell you if there is more water beyond your vision. They can only tell you that there is apparently water at the end of the landmass on which you are currently located. Even if you go swimming in the water you will not know for sure if there is more water outside the scope of your vision. So what? Maybe you are happy with the amount of the ocean that you can see. If that is the case with your life, if your life is already so happy that you neither need nor can imagine being any happier, then devotion to God might not seem very important.

If, on the other hand, you are not happy with your life and the ups and downs in life are making you a bit nauseous, perhaps you have caught onto the fact that no happiness in this world will either completely fulfill you or last more than a temporary length of time. As a result, the idea of finding a permanent source of happiness will be very attractive.

Here is a story to illustrate:

There was a loving couple who lost their child in the forest one day. The parents called to the child constantly without stopping. Day and night they called to their child but there was no response.

The child had wandered away from its parents in search fun. Finding one entertainment after another the child walked deeper and deeper into the forest; becoming so involved with play that it did not hear its parents calling for it to come home.

Five Virtues of the Positive Flow

Eventually the fun that the child had been having turned to boredom. Then the child was sad. Sitting forlorn the child listened to the sounds of the forest and began to think that maybe there was a voice calling in the distance. Just then some more fun appeared so the child played and ignored the distant call.

All the while, the parents kept calling for their child.

Eventually the child became bored and sad again. It was quiet in the forest and after listening for a long time the child was sure that there was someone calling from a distance. The child called out to the distant voice, "I'm over here. Please come and help me!"

Instantly the parents heard the child's voice and began to run through the forest. There were no thoughts of reproach or anger in the minds of the parents, only love. They loved their child and longed to be reunited again.

Whenever the parents could hear the child calling out, they would run towards the sound. When the child was distracted by other things, they would wait patiently in hopes of hearing the child's voice again. Once they heard the voice they would again run towards it.

Eventually after a very long time, the child called out and didn't stop. Once that constant call was resounding in the forest the parents could quickly find their child. When the parents and child were finally reunited the child was so happy that it thought, "Why did I take so long to call out? I can't believe I thought that playing in the forest was more fun than bathing in the love of my parents."

God is our Father/Mother and has been calling for us to come home. We, on the other hand, have been listening to the sounds of this world and not the inner sounds of the Divine Presence. Our various attempts, whether conscious or unconscious, to tap into the energies of the positive flow have put our Creator ever closer at hand. For every step that we take towards God, God moves towards us a hundredfold. In order to close that final gap we need to broadcast our desire to play no more in the world, but to live once again in the infinite arms of love and joy. There is no reproach in God's desire for us to be reunited in Spirit. There is only the infinite love, bliss and peace of Spirit which is the foundation of all existence.

Devotion to God - no matter what name we want to attach to Infinite Spirit - puts our efforts to be in tune with the positive flow into overdrive. Through the inner expression of our love for the source and substance of love itself we become magnetically charged with the kind of love that God cannot fail to hear and respond to.

God not only wants to come to us, but must come to us through the very laws that He/She made. So don't just call, "Oh, I wonder if you, God, aren't too busy, if you could maybe help me out and give me eternal happiness?" Call with all of the urgency of a drowning person seeking air. Call to God with every fiber of your being and respectfully demand, as a child of the Infinite, that the Divine Presence be made known to you! Let there be no mistaking the urgency or resolve of your efforts to contact your Creator.

Chapter 10
Creativity and Materializing Your Dreams

I mentioned earlier that the positive flow is the source of all creativity. Let's talk about why this is true. In order to do so we must go back to the concept that all of life is projected first through the causal - or ideational - plane.

The causal plane is where all of the ideas that become the astral and physical planes originate. Everything in life; from the creation of star systems to the ability to think that it might be nice to cross the street or scratch the back of your head is rooted in the thought creations of the causal plane. If we can think it, the potential for that thought comes from the causal plane.

This brings us to an incredible truth: All thoughts are universally rooted. That means the source of all of the knowledge as expressed by all people is not found in each individual's brain but in the central storehouse of knowledge in the causal plane. Why do different people have different thoughts? Because we each tune in differently to that central source.

If you were at a huge warehouse filled with house wares you would find that the people coming in to find things would choose different items. Even though all of the items in the warehouse are available to all, not everyone is interested in everything. People looking for ceramic dishes may be totally uninterested in potato peelers. It is also true that when we limit our view only to that which is right in front of us we simply do not see other possibilities. In addition, the negative flow encourages us to believe that if we can't see it, it doesn't exist.

The universal storehouse of knowledge is so large that most of it simply does not pertain to the circumstances of our daily lives. Yet all of that knowledge is theoretically available to us even if we are not interested in checking it out at this time. As a practical matter most of us have not developed our ability to consciously tap this source, but that does not mean we couldn't if we tried.

So if we are not consciously tapping this storehouse of thoughts, how do we get the thoughts that we do have?

Magnetism

We magnetically draw thoughts that are in tune with the magnetism of our consciousness. All of that thought potential is always there (remember, Spirit is center everywhere) but the thoughts that we end up perceiving are the ones that are drawn to us through the qualities of energy that we are radiating.

If we are angry, we draw thoughts that support anger. If we are peaceful we draw thoughts compatible with peace. If we think a lot about math we will draw more thoughts about the subject. If we try to imagine a new design for a car, house or boat, new possible designs will begin to flow towards us.

Another aspect of this is not only the subject matter but the direction of our consciousness overall. If we are radiating the consciousness of expansion then new creative thoughts will present themselves to us. When we think in contractive terms, like doing things the same old way, we will limit the thoughts that we draw to those same old ways. This is one of the reasons why it is so helpful to maintain an expansive outlook towards life.

New possibilities and potentials will present themselves only to minds that expansively attract them. It is like any talent or ability that you might have, if you want to be good at it you need to practice what you know and continually seek fresh ways to improve and expand on your present abilities.

Creativity & Materializing Your Dreams

In order to receive creative solutions to any question, situation or area of endeavor what we need to do is apply our formula. First we observe that there is an area of need or interest. Then we focus the broadcast of our need as specifically or generally, as we feel is appropriate for the situation. Remember, the more specific our request the more specific the results. The immediacy of the response will depend on the amount and the focus of our energy, and our openness to receiving the response.

Some situations require immediate solutions. In cases like that you will with practice draw an immediate response. Don't expect the Red Sea to part on your first day out. At the same time, do not leave the possibility out either. If you doubt that an answer can come you will be less able to perceive one if it does.

Not all of your broadcasts for help will need instant answers. When you do not get one right away continue broadcasting at regular intervals for periods of time that work for you. You could try five minutes out of every hour, one hour a day for a week or whatever you feel is appropriate for the situation. Experiment with intervals and levels of intensity; this is also a part of the formula.

Some situations will take years of regular attempts to receive a satisfactory answer while others will draw an immediate response. As your life moves forward in harmony with the positive flow the answers to your inner broadcasts will come in their own time and that will be the right time. So apply the elevating qualities of persistence and patience to your efforts and leave the results to the wisdom of the positive flow.

You can cultivate the ability to receive inner inspiration by the practice of inwardly listening even when you do not need a specific answer. Let's say you are at the office and someone asks you a question. If you are not already consciously connected to your heart and spiritual eye as a part of your current consciousness connect right away. If you can, get connected before the person asks their question. Otherwise, connect while they are talking. It doesn't take long to connect once you know what it feels like. Then listen to the question as if it were entering directly into your inner connection, without filtering it with your own thought reactions. Let it flow right up to your spiritual eye. By doing this you are redirecting the energy from receiving it in your ego to acting as a channel for its presentation to the positive flow.

Practice will acclimatize you to the process and develop your ability to be inwardly connected and receive answers. The idea is to begin living this way all of the time: at the grocery store, when you play sports, while you cook and eat your meals, while you listen to music, while you do everything in your life. This is your inner connection to the positive flow and the more you use the connection the better you will be at it.

The answers that you receive will sometimes just pop into your mind like a very clear thought. Sometimes as you begin discussing a subject your thoughts will gradually clarify into a feeling of correctness. You may find that as you are talking a new idea will just pop out into your conversation. Remember, it is a flow. As you work with your inner connection be open and ever watchful for the creative ways that new understandings can come to you.

Sometimes you will find the answers flowing to you through others. As you talk to them they will share an idea and you will inwardly feel the correctness of their words. You may even find that while others are talking about things that have nothing to do with the answer you are seeking, their words are heard by you in a way that answers your question. There is no limit to the variety of ways that new understanding can come.

The positive flow can and does speak to us through all of life. We can find new inspirations coming to us through the most unexpected of channels - a barking dog, a screeching tire, the patterns on an old rock wall, a pile of trash lying in the street. This is why the *Way of the Positive Flow* requires continuous attention to our inner relationship with life.

Creativity & Materializing Your Dreams

Through the constant cultivation of this inner relationship you will find the positive flow to be your best of friends - always with you, never judgmental, silent at times when you are not open to hearing a helpful word and ever full of loving support. You will also find that this inner guidance has a sense of humor. So don't be afraid to laugh when the universe decides to share a joke with you!

Along with this willingness to support you is the power to help you realize your dreams, whatever they may be. Of course, if you dream for something unrealistic you may not achieve your goal this time around, but the law of cause and effect will eventually bring all of your desires to fulfillment. Keeping that in mind, take care what you dream for!

There is nothing out of harmony with the positive flow when you have innocent desires. These are things that are of personal interest to you that do not get in the way of your overall movement towards infinite expansion. Traveling to a far off place, a night at the opera, putting together a family reunion, going to the Superbowl, becoming a proficient athlete in your chosen area of interest, are all examples of things that, all things being equal, are not going to seriously get you off track.

Trouble areas might be the desire to have fame or wealth. Revenge on old enemies would not be a very helpful dream. Anything associated with downward-pulling energies is something to be avoided. If you have a dream of this type, try to redirect that energy into a positive direction. Conquer the power of vengeful thoughts by helping people who have hurt you. Conquer the desire for personal fame by helping someone else to become famous. These endeavors redirect the energy in ways that are helpful to you, while simultaneously helping you to avoid sowing seeds that will sprout negative results in your future.

Once you have identified an area of interest apply your outward and inward energies towards the manifestation of your dream. Form a clear picture in your mind of what it is you are trying to achieve. Visualize yourself having attained your goal. Imagine what it is like having arrived at your dream. This helps you to clearly fix an idea in your mind and to start energizing it. It also helps you to double check and make sure that this dream is worth receiving the amount of energy that it will take to manifest it.

When my daughter Sabari was about eleven or twelve years old she came home one day saying that she wanted a horse. She had been participating in a pony club and some of the other girls had gotten their own horses. It seemed like a good idea to her.

My own enthusiasm for the idea wasn't very high but I did not want to dampen her interest if it was genuine. I discussed the situation with her and I asked Sabari to tell me what it would be like having a horse.

Sabari then began to describe all of the areas of involvement that would be a part of owning a horse. At first she talked with enthusiasm about every detail but as those details began to add up she started to lose steam. By the time we were done she realized that having a horse was a lot more than just riding it once in a while.

I suggested that she think about it some more before making a decision. A few days later she told me that she didn't think she really wanted to put that much energy into it and that she would continue with the way things were.

The process of entering into her dream made it real and practical for her. We need to do the same thing before we launch ourselves into a direction that we may not be able to complete. We also may save ourselves much exertion by realizing that we would not have enjoyed the results of our efforts once we got there. Practicality is also a part of the positive flow.

At the same time, do not let the difficulty or even seeming impossibility of a dream keep you from thoroughly exploring the possibilities before you give up. Most of the great inventions and adventures that people have embarked on in history were considered impossible at the time. It is also true that the achievement of most goals is not what trying is all about. It is the effort and the process of working against all odds that challenges our inner spirit. After all, what is impossible to the Creator of life who is seeking to have an adventure through us?

Balanced fanaticism is the key to success in the achievement of our dreams. We need to approach our dreams with an even mind and an indomitable spirit. Those two together can achieve goals well beyond that which the common mind considers possible. Through attunement to the positive flow during every step of the way we will begin to find doors opening that we never could have anticipated. Life is so dynamically connected that our minds simply cannot grasp the concept fully.

I remember hitchhiking in New Zealand in 1970. I was sitting on a very isolated road sticking my thumb out at cars that came by at the rate of about one every hour and a half. I had been there for three or four hours and my patience was more than a little lagging. I began to think what horrible people those folks who did not pick me up must have been. I was also feeling sorry for myself. As I built up steam I began to ponder all that is unjust in the world. I had a classic case of the negative flow making a mountain out of a mole hill!

Then I remembered this idea that all of life is connected. It occurred to me that the reason I had not been picked up yet was that the right people were on their way, but had not yet arrived. Within half an hour of that thought process a van stopped to pick me up. Not only were they going right to where I wanted to go, but I discovered that we had mutual friends in the United States. Is that amazing? What are the chances of being picked up on the other side of the world by people who are friends of a friend?

If this were an isolated story I might be able to see the possibility of "coincidence". However I have experienced, as have many others whom I know, that these things happen all of

Way of the Positive Flow

the time. Why do they happen? Because we are all connected; in fact, we are all one.

Do not be afraid to apply the resources of the positive flow to materialize your dreams within this larger dream that we call life. There is no more practical approach to succeeding in life than consciously aligning our efforts with the ideas and energies of the universe.

Chapter 11
Through Many Lives

Throughout our discussion I have hinted at a subject that pulls much of what we have been talking about into a cohesive whole. At the same time, it is not necessary to accept the ideas in this chapter to apply the techniques we have covered. So keep that in mind as we launch ourselves into concepts that explain much about who we are and how we got this way.

While our larger reality is that of infinite Spirit, most of us are only aware of the limited circumstances of this physical world. How is it that we ended up in this time and place on this planet, born into one family and not another, with the specific talents and tendencies that seem to have come with the form that we now inhabit?

We can surmise from our earlier discussion that it was our magnetism that drew us to all of the specifics of our circumstances, but how did we get the particular qualities of magnetism that we have?

Every religion has its own take on the origins of life and the evolution of the soul. For each of us, the important part of any explanation is how we can use it to live life successfully while facing the fact that life in these physical bodies will one day end. Our biggest problem is that, barring a personal vision of universal knowledge, we will not know for sure how things work until we die. So we are stuck with accepting someone else's story - or believing none of them - until we can experience our own.

The following explanation of the origin of the soul is based on the ancient teachings of India and provides a workable framework from which we can make sense out of how life works and how we got where we are today.

When a part of infinite Spirit becomes individualized it is described as a soul. This individualized Spirit first experiences itself as part of the mineral kingdom. Through eons of time the soul gradually works its way up the ladder of physical evolution. In each progressive stage the soul has ever greater ability to express higher levels of awareness. This is the expanding of consciousness through the physical creation: from rocks, to single celled life, to insects, to invertebrate and then vertebrate animals and finally to mammals. The human form is the peak of physical evolution.

During the early part of the journey the soul has little or no control of its destiny - the transmigration of the soul through progressively more advanced forms is a fairly automatic process. It is only once we get to the human form that we can begin to consciously work toward hastening or delaying our progress back to infinite consciousness.

Once in the human form the soul takes on the ego - the soul identified with the body. The ego carries our likes and dislikes. We also carry within us the seeds of past actions, both positive and negative. It is these inner commitments of energy that bind us to the ups and downs of this physical plane.

Before evolving to the human form animals simply are what they are. They do not have a self-consciousness that has feelings about how they feel. According to the abilities of their form they are conscious and experience pleasure and pain, love and hate. While animals can create attachments to the feelings that they have, those attachments do not cling to the soul through incarnations the same way as after the soul attains the human form.

Through Many Lives

An animal that has been mistreated will respond relatively quickly to loving attention. A human being that has been mistreated may go incarnations without completely releasing those negative feelings. This is one of the reasons some people think that animals are more advanced than people. Certainly their ability to let things go is a quality that we should try to emulate, but animals can not realize their infinite beginnings. They do not have the complex cerebral and spinal energy centers that animate the human form. These centers are necessary for the channeling of the fantastic amount of energy that is involved in the process of Self-realization.

In the beginning of our human experiences all we care about is eating, sleeping and procreating. This gradually expands to other areas, guided by the basic principle of seeking what is enjoyable and avoiding that which is unpleasant.

The difficulty in making progress once the human form has been achieved is our identification with the senses and our desire to enjoy life through them. To make it even more convoluted, as we experience things in life we create likes and dislikes about everything. We like sweets, we like sex, we like power, we like fame, we do not like sickness, we do not like being left out of the "in" crowd, we do not like feeling alone. These fluctuations in the mind are indicative of our immersion in our physicality. It takes many, many incarnations before we begin to wake up to the idea that there is more going on in life than the mere seeking of pleasure and avoidance of pain.

By the time we decide to seek greater understanding about how to live in harmony with life we are carrying the baggage of all our past incarnations. In the last chapter I mentioned that it was a good idea to be careful about what one desires. This is because all of our desires must be fulfilled. If you desire to murder someone and you don't get to do it in this life you will have to come back and do it in another. If you want to be a king, queen, hero, scientist, magician, tyrant or whatever, you will have to come back to experience it.

Way of the Positive Flow

In the beginning that might not seem like such a bad deal. You get to fulfill all of your fantasies. The whole creation is God's big huge holographic movie that has an incredible amount of twists and turns in the plot. Everyone gets to be the hero/heroine at one time or another. Of course we also have to play the slave, the mistreated and the handicapped. We will most certainly be visited by disease and despair. So after, say a few million incarnations, things start to get repetitious. After all, even being a king can get old after a few thousand tries!

Eventually the soul gets weary of all these ups and downs and begins to search for an end to its part in the movie. Once that desire comes it too must be fulfilled. At that point the soul, relative to how long it has been away from its home in Spirit, is very near the end of its journey.

Now that the soul has decided to seek an end to birth, death and rebirth, it finds that it is bound by many desires from the past. These desires are carried in the astral body and go with the soul from one physical incarnation to the next. These past commitments of energy are what make up the totality of our magnetism. They determine where we are and how we got here.

In order to release ourselves from our past we need to do two things. The first is to stop making new commitments that we will have to work out in the future. Second, we want to release the energies of the past without having to experience each and every one of them individually.

The way to deal with the first issue is to live in this world without attachment. If an angry thought comes through your mind don't hold onto it. Remember, a thought is not yours until you attach yourself to it. You magnetically drew the thought as a potential reaction to a situation and you can choose not to accept it. The more successful you are at letting negative thoughts go through you without clinging to them, the more you will find that they do not come because they are not welcome. When they stop coming altogether you will know that you have truly changed the quality of your magnetism.

This idea of not attaching yourself to things works with all areas of life. When you can experience life not with indifference but with the positive elevating qualities that we have been discussing, negative energies will not be able to stick in your consciousness.

In order to get rid of our past commitments of energy - our karma - we need to increase the upward flow of energy in the spine towards the spiritual eye. The higher techniques of meditation work directly with this inner flow and are designed to speed up our release from the past.

The technique of Kriya Yoga, as introduced in America by Paramhansa Yogananda, is the technique that I am most familiar with. The important thing to look for when seeking a meditation technique is to find one that has a history of success. If you find a technique that has produced a long line of saints, who have used that technique to achieve freedom from the cycles of birth, death and rebirth, then there is a good chance that the technique could work for you as well.

There are many people teaching meditation today and claims of all kinds are made. Use the positive flow to direct you to the right technique for you. That is the best way to be assured that you are making the right choice for your life.

The concept of reincarnation makes sense out of the seeming arbitrariness of life. It puts the miseries of some and the pleasures of others into a perspective that actually makes sense. All of nature around us has order. There is a natural ebb and flow to the way nature moves one way and then the next. Does it seem possible that any part of life could be separate from that natural order?

How could a Mozart or a DiVinci come into this world with so much creative talent unless it was brought forth as the result of previously developed talents from former incarnations? How can a good natured child spring forth from mean-hearted parents? Certainly the ideas of heredity would mean that all of the children of mean parents would be mean themselves.

Way of the Positive Flow

Unless, I suppose, one were to describe the kind-hearted child as a mutant!

On a more personal note, doesn't this make sense in the light of how we feel inside? Don't we experience impulses that we just cannot attribute to our upbringing?

For what it is worth, all of the great religious traditions throughout history have included the teaching of reincarnation. In the East it is clearly a part of all the major traditions. In the West, church authorities have tried to expunge it from the Christian tradition, but if you look for it you can still find traces of it.

The greatest value that the idea of reincarnation has for us is that it puts our present circumstances into a perspective that we can work with. As I said in the beginning, the *Way of the Positive Flow* is not about theories. We want practical, personally verifiable results from our efforts. We can use the idea of reincarnation to give us information the way a map would, but ultimately, we can only believe in the map once we have arrived at our destination. Having arrived we can say for ourselves that the map was correct.

The Buddha was once asked why we should love all persons equally. He responded, "Because in the very numerous and varied life spans of each man, every other being has at one time or another been dear to him."

It has been a long journey for all of us. Let us take heart in the thought that we are now on our way home. We are returning to our infinite source to rest once again on the bosom of ever-new love and joy.

Through Many Lives
by Swami Kriyananda

Through many lives I've drunk the cup of laughter,
No man could tell the pleasures I have known.
The stars in the endless sky
If one could count would come to billions.
Yet as vast as are their numbers,
So many years I've wandered far from You.

Through many lives I've drunk the cup of sorrow:
No man could tell the bitter tears I've shed.
The drops in the mighty sea
If one could count would come to billions
Yet as vast as are their numbers,
So many years I've wandered far from You.

Through countless lives
I sought Your cup of sweetness,
Found other cups, yet thirsted evermore.
The streams in the hills of time
All found their way into a desert;
Every noon of bright fulfillment
Ere many hours did sink to evening gloom.

I long for You in summer and in winter,
Only for You my heart thirsts day and night.
I've learned that the fairest songs
Ears ever heard were but Your echo.
Lord, at last fill me completely,
For nevermore I'd wander far from You.

Chapter 12
Choosing Your World

The world in which we live appears very different to its many human inhabitants. An aborigine in the bush of Australia could very well be living on a different planet than a socialite in New York City. Mine workers who dig in underground tunnels have a very different view than iron workers who build skyscrapers. On the surface of life everything seems diverse, different and disconnected. Underneath the surface we find that life is more about how we are all uniquely the same.

Most people don't even realize that we each have a question to answer about our lives. What part of this world will each of us choose to live in? I am not referring as much to the outward circumstances of our lives, as the inner view that we each have of life. No matter what the circumstances in which we find ourselves the view of life that we have is up to us. It is the classic question that the Zen Master will ask the student after handing him/her a glass half filled with water "Is this glass half empty? Or half full?"

One of the most valuable lessons of the teaching of reincarnation is that we are all responsible for the world in which we find ourselves. God has not just whimsically thrown us into our current situation. We were each drawn here by the sum total of our past actions and reactions. We have consciously or unconsciously chosen our current circumstances.

Choosing Your World

Once we have accepted that we can have an effect on the way our lives proceed we need to decide whether we are going to participate actively or passively. The *Way of the Positive Flow* is about consciously entering into the process of living. We no longer want to be passive about our lives. Regardless of our past we can improve our future by living each moment of the present in the best possible way. We are the creators of our own lives and the way to create the results that we would prefer in life is to make conscious choices.

Take a moment to think about the way that you react to life. When you walk down the street what do you see first, that which is beautiful or that which is dirty? When you meet someone new, do you see their good traits first or do you see their faults? When you find yourself in a new situation are you more concerned about what you can get or what you can give? When you face a new challenge do you think "Oh, what a hassle." or do you say "I can't wait to start!"

How do you react to criticism? Do you judge people by their outward appearance alone? How do you deal with praise? If there was a high unemployment rate and you needed a job would you be optimistic or pessimistic? When you witness the good fortune of others are you genuinely happy for them? Or are you more concerned about what it would be like if it had happened to you?

Certainly our reactions to life are not as black and white as some of these questions, but they do illustrate the directions that our consciousness tends to take. And that brings us to this important point: It is the direction of our consciousness that controls the choices that we make in life.

If our consciousness is attuned to the positive flow we will make choices that lead us towards beneficial results, even if we cannot see those results at the time we act. If we make choices that are based in the energies of the negative flow we will find that even though we might receive short term gains, in the long run those choices will be to our detriment.

Way of the Positive Flow

There was once a waitress in a small restaurant. An older man came in to eat there on a regular basis. The man was somewhat tattered looking but the waitress always treated him with respect. Over a period of time they chatted and became friendly towards one another. The waitress never saw the man outside of the restaurant and the man never left more than a small tip.

One day the old man stopped coming to the restaurant. Occasionally the waitress would wonder what had happened to the old man. A few months later the waitress received a large check in the mail. The old man had died. In his will was a large bequest to her as an expression of his appreciation for her kindness.

If the waitress had thought only of the short term and had not been friendly to the old man, not wanting to be bothered with him because of his tattered appearance, she would have been expressing a low energy, negative attitude instead of a high energy, positive attitude. Our lives are constantly filled with opportunities to grow in our connection with the positive flow. By reacting to all life experiences with positive energies we are aligning our consciousness with the magnetic powers of the positive flow. This is what is actually going on beneath the surface of our lives.

There are many different ways that unselfish kindness comes back to bless us in the future but a much more important benefit to acting consistently with a consciousness of kindness is that we get to live on a daily basis in the vibration of kindness.

When we live in the positive flow we live in a positive magnetism that provides an aura of peace, joy and well-being that we can experience no matter where we are or what we are doing. This is the world that we really want to live in. Our own portable paradise of inner connection to life's wellspring of goodness is the real pot of gold at the end of the rainbow.

Of course, the problem is that life challenges us in ways that make it difficult to feel inner peace. It is not easy

84

to feel peaceful when you just lost a sale that you spent months developing and that would have set you up financially for months or years to come. Peace can seem an impossible dream when you realize your kids just broke a valuable family keepsake or when your spouse of many years announces that it is time to move on.

Having the right attitude toward life is not like putting money in the bank. We can't go through life reserving the right attitude for that one big moment when we will pull it out of our savings on a rainy day. Life is like sports or business. We need to exert consistent effort to express a positive energy in all situations and then apply those efforts to ever greater challenges. Only then can we expect to be fit enough to face life's greatest challenges with equanimity.

What does this add up to? The way to find the grace to live well in the big moments of our lives is to live well in all of the little moments.

There is actually a lot that we can do along the way to improve our lives both inwardly and outwardly as we work our way forward. And it is work! It can be happy work or sad work - depending on how we choose to look at things. But it will be work. It is not easy to transform ourselves into our highest potential. Olympic athletes know what it takes to produce an ever-increasing personal best. They apply levels of determination that inspire us all. That is what we want to be: Olympians in the sport of life.

When you start yourself going in the right direction, no matter how slow things seem to be proceeding, if you keep pushing forward the goal will be reached. Set yourself a training schedule that includes intense sessions of immersion in positively magnetic energy (like meditation) and look at your life with the goal of harmonizing each area with the ultimate goal of self-realization. If there is an area in your life that is keeping you from attaining your goal then adjust that situation or cut it out altogether.

Way of the Positive Flow

Make no mistake about it; if you want to reach the heights of your potential the climb will be the most challenging effort of your life, but the rewards will also be the most uplifting. Along the way you will experience the most amazing thing: happiness.

When we live our lives tuning in to ever deeper levels of the positive flow we won't need to wait until the end of life to find out if our efforts are working. We will experience right here and now an inner peace, joy and happiness that will leave no room for doubt that life, at its core, is truly beautiful and unending.

In the coming chapters we will be discussing different areas of life and how to use the positive flow to increase outward and inward success. It is important to remember that it is the underlying approach to life that we want to focus on and not the specifics that are used to illustrate these principles. Once you have gotten the idea of how this works firmly in your mind, you will know how to find the specific choices that meet the needs of your own life.

While it is true that expansion into the infinite bliss of Spirit is our ultimate goal, the practical attainment of that goal hinges on how we live the day to day challenges that we now face. So let's explore how we can transform the landscape of our consciousness into a garden of never-ending peace and joy.

Chapter 13
The Diet
of Your Life

There is a saying: You are what you eat. In this chapter we are going to expand that concept to: You are what you take in through all of your faculties of perception. While it is ultimately true that we are Spirit and not the body or mind that we now experience, we still need the abilities of the body and mind in order to reach beyond them and realize our deeper identity. Just like any builder or artist we will want to sharpen our tools and maintain them in good working order so that they do not prevent us from doing our best work.

On one hand our diet is an issue of nourishment. On the other hand diet can be that which we do not eat in order to maintain our health. The diet of a person who is trying to live in the positive flow of life takes into account both of these ideas and applies them to the underlying energies behind what we take into our physical, mental/emotional and spiritual bodies. By regulating our intake we nourish ourselves while at the same time avoiding those things that are not beneficial to us.

We are not going to focus only on food here. We are going to explore some ideas that will open up new frontiers in the way that you approach what you eat, where you eat and how you eat. Once you have a grasp on what we are trying to do you will be able to apply these ideas not only to your food intake, but to the energies that you take in during all life experiences.

Way of the Positive Flow

One of the common approaches to life is: If it feels good, do it!

As we have discussed how things that feel good at the time often lead to unpleasant repercussions down the road. Sometimes the most bitter food or medicine is just what we need for healing or growth. So how do we decide what to take into ourselves?

Guess what? We apply our formula!

How do we get the ball rolling? Well, we have already talked about how everything in life is an expression of one or a mixture of the three qualities: elevating, activating or downward-pulling. When we want to decide if something is good for us we tune into its vibration. Is it elevating, activating or downward-pulling? Once we know its vibration we can decide if it is something that we want to make a part of our own vibration.

In order to do this we have to establish our inner connection with the positive flow. From that inner perspective we can reach out to feel the essential vibration of whatever we are evaluating. Observe everything in this inner light. Try to reach out and be that which you are looking at. Then attune yourself to the positive flow for greater understanding about the vibrations that you are feeling. Once you have done that, experiment.

Try this at first with things that are not going to make that much difference one way or the other. See if your inner impression before you take in the experience is anything like how you feel during and after the experience.

Here is an experiment that you can try the next time you go out to eat at a restaurant.

Find a street that has many restaurants on it. Look at the buildings and try to feel the vibrations of what it would be like inside. Then go into several of them and see if the outside feeling fits the inside feeling. After that, choose a restaurant that has the feeling you like the most and eat there. When you are done eating evaluate how you feel about the totality of the experience. Was it uplifting, activating, downward-pulling or a mixture of all three? If it was a mixture of energies - which is most likely - which energy was predominant? Be sure that you inwardly reach out beyond your senses to intuitively read the energies around and within you.

Remember to connect your thoughts during the evaluation to the positive flow. New ideas may present themselves to you as you evaluate your experience. If you could feel the positive flow before the experience but not afterward; try to figure out when and why you lost your connection. It could be one particular part of your experience or it could be the sum total.

By approaching all of your life this way you will learn how to recognize the energies underneath the exterior of life that you experience through the senses. You will also begin to see how your own energies are changed by all of the different types of stimulation that are taken in each day. The state of the soul is greatly affected by the type of diet that it is fed through the body, mind and emotions.

If business or good manners requires you to go into an environment that you know is downward-pulling, protect yourself by staying firmly connected to the positive flow. Avoid eating if you can. If you must, then eat the least amount possible. In this way you will maximize the strength of your ability to repel the negative or restless vibrations and minimize their effect on you.

When it comes to food people have different tastes and different bodily needs. While we can generalize about nutrition as it pertains to all bodies, it is essential that we each tune in to the specific needs and preferences that belong to our own particular body.

The more subtle aspects of what we eat are: the vibration of the food itself, the vibration of the way it is prepared, the vibration of the way it is served and the vibration of the way it is eaten. All of these factors are part of how we are affected by the experience.

Elevating foods are full of life force. They are vital with energy and nutrition. Fruits and nuts are the most elevating foods. Fresh vegetables, whole grains, fresh unpasteurized milk and yogurt are also elevating. Don't forget the importance of sunlight and fresh air, which provide nutrients that the body absorbs as both physical and subtle energies.

Activating foods are those that stimulate us. Spices, caffeine, sugar, salt and foods high in protein all have activating energy.

Downward-pulling foods are those that are lacking in life force. They have low nutritional value and/or negative energies in them. Examples of this would be: highly processed foods, old or rotten food, food that includes a lot of chemical additives, food that is overcooked or sitting too long after cooking, food that has been stored too long, food that was prepared by a person with negative energies (this is always a risk when you eat out) and food that tastes bad.

Are you wondering why bad tasting food is downward-pulling? In order to absorb the life force and nutrient value of a food it is necessary for the body to open itself up to receiving that value. If the food tastes too bad the body may even physically reject it by regurgitating it. On the other hand, when food tastes good the body relaxes and opens itself up to proper digestion. I'm not suggesting that we should be overly attached to the way things taste; I am saying we should eat the right things in the right amount and enjoy our food while we are eating it.

The odor of food also affects us the way taste does. Have you ever tried to eat something that smells bad? The body instinctively cringes at the odor and the stomach muscles tighten as a strong signal towards rejection. If you know that a food or medicine is good for you, you may need to pinch your nose in order to eat it. As a general practice try to eat foods that have a pleasant aroma.

The Diet of Your Life

After a good meal the body and mind should feel light, fulfilled and energetic. If you find that after eating you have trouble thinking, feel like going to sleep, feel agitated in your mind, can't sit still or feel a heaviness in your stomach; something about what you ate, how much of it you ate or where and the way that you ate it was downward-pulling. Looking at all of these factors will help you to evaluate the situation. You will also want to check your connection to the positive flow. There is a very high probability that you became disconnected at some point.

When people eat red meat, fowl and fish they are taking in food that ranges from very downward-pulling to a mixture of downward-pulling and activating. It is true that fresh meat is stimulating (activating) to the body, but it also has toxins that pull the body down along with negative energies associated with the killing of the animal. Of the three, fish is the least downward-pulling and then fowl. Pork and red meat are on the bottom of the list of things to eat. For people who are trying to raise the vibration of their consciousness it is best to avoid eating meat.

A vegetarian diet is the most practical for living in the positive flow. A fruitarian diet is actually the most elevating but most of us won't as a practical matter be able to maintain that type of diet considering the way that we live. If we were living away from society in a very elevating environment then a fruitarian diet would be an advantageous way to eat. Since we do live in a very active society we need foods that will elevate us while also providing the activating energies that are necessary for doing our work in the world. A reasonably well-balanced vegetarian diet will provide us with good nutrition and elevating vibrations.

I remember when I became a vegetarian as a teenager. Almost everyone I knew thought I was going to die. People used to look at me like I was crazy. Now you can get vegetarian dishes in the majority of restaurants. Why? Because scientific research has shown that eating meat is not as healthy as people once thought.

The goal is to find a simple diet that feels comfortable to your body and then follow it without being obsessive. There is too much to do elsewhere to worry excessively about what we eat. Some people think that just by eating good foods they are growing spiritually. Well, it may be true to some small degree, but it may also be true for them that their over interest in what they eat is in itself a downward-pulling energy. A simple, balanced diet, fine tuned by our inspirations from the positive flow will suffice to power the body and minimize the negative energies that sometimes come in through the process of fueling these physical forms.

These ideas also pertain to what we drink. Sodas and other highly processed and artificially sweetened drinks are low in vitality and long on stimulants and unhealthy chemicals. When possible choose fresh fruit juices and clean spring or well water because these are the most elevating.

Coffee and tea that contain caffeine are not only stimulating but potentially addicting. Try herbal teas and save coffees and teas with caffeine for special occasions.

Again, where we eat also affects us. If the environment that we are eating in is elevating our bodies and minds will be calm and relaxed; better able to absorb the hopefully elevating qualities of the food. If there is loud music, people yelling or arguing, babies crying at the top of their lungs, discussion of unpleasant subjects, lots of people scurrying around or any other agitating energy, we won't be able to receive the meal properly because we will be inwardly defending ourselves from all of those tumultuous energies.

Eat in a calm and cheerful environment. Have sufficient lighting so that you can see your food. Music at mealtime should not be so stimulating that it makes you want to tap your foot to the beat. Pleasant company with friendly conversation is beneficial; so also is silence. The room should not be too warm or stuffy, so that you can breathe easily. Clean dishes and utensils that are pleasant to look at are elevating. Laughter at the table is also good as it stimulates the stomach area and lightens the spirit. These are just a few examples of areas to look at when evaluating your eating environment. Taking the time to consciously look at these things helps us to see what is going on in our lives (observation) so that we can then come up with ways to improve things (attunement) and work towards (experiment) making things better.

Also consider how you eat. Gulping your food or drink, slouching, chewing quickly, hoarding the best servings, drinking too much while eating, talking loudly, arguing, moving around too much in your chair and chewing with your mouth open are examples of downward-pulling energies at the table. Some elevating examples would be: chewing your food well from bites that are not too big, sitting upright in your chair without fidgeting, using good table manners, speaking and listening with good natured attentiveness, eating in silence, smiling, offering to pass others some of the dishes, giving others the best portion, not eating too much or too little, and of course saving a little room for dessert!

By paying attention to all of these aspects of food in our lives we will find that eating can be a pleasure that will not create the need for a balancing negative energy. We will also find our efforts in this area reaching out to other parts of our life.

Apply these ideas to the other senses as well. Use your attunement to the positive flow to discover how you are affected by every outward stimulation in your life. Then begin to consciously choose the experiences that you find uplifting and avoid or minimize those that you find downward-pulling.

Let's not forget to add to our inner and outer diet the spice of thankfulness. This elevates our attention to the source of life and reminds us that all of the bounty in our lives is given to us by our Creator. Even the bitter herbs of life are gifts that cleanse us along our path. Each and every breath, our very

Way of the Positive Flow

power to move forward in life is given to us as an opportunity to come closer to our home in Spirit. Life in the positive flow is about experiencing our connection to Spirit as the most essential food. When we live with a steady diet of inner connectedness to the positive flow we will find that we are receiving the most essential nourishment of all – the loving companionship of Infinite Spirit.

Chapter 14
Sights, Sounds & Inspiration

Just like the food we eat the sights, sounds and thoughts that we take in from the world around us can lift us up and nourish our highest aspirations or they can pull us down and bind our souls to the limitations of this physical world. Deciding what we take into our consciousness through music, movies and television is every bit as important as what we take in physically at mealtime.

When I was in elementary school I played the clarinet and then the viola in our school orchestra. My mother took me to operas and musicals, of which my favorites were the opera "Carmen" and the musical "The Man of La Mancha." I also sang in several choirs during those years. I loved the power that music had to connect me with forces that were larger than those that I could feel by myself.

When the Beatles appeared on the American music scene that was pretty much the end of my love affair with classical music. I turned in my viola for strings of a different sort: the guitar. Rock and roll and then later the blues became the forms of music that most expressed and molded the emotions that flew through the storm of my teenage awareness. And of course to my parents dismay, the louder the better!

In the late summer of 1967 when I was fifteen years old, my parents took our family on vacation to Carmel,

Way of the Positive Flow

California. During our visit my older brother and sister heard about a concert in nearby Monterey. The concert was a three day music extravaganza called the Monterey Pop Festival. So my folks dropped us off at the gate one afternoon and picked us up around midnight. Not only did they have no idea what their children were about to experience, neither did their children.

The sights and sounds of that day are indelibly etched in my mind. Swirling odors of incense, marijuana (I had no idea what it was at the time), perfumes and sweat all mixed with the colorful garments - or lack thereof - of the flower children. Tents and booths with displays of handmade crafts seemed like the market place from a far off planet. I had never seen so many men with flowing locks down their backs and women dressed in wild colors with flowers in their hair.

Everyone I met that day was smiling and friendly. It was like we were all one big happy family, meeting relatives that we hadn't yet had the chance to meet. I felt like a puppy with his eyes wide, not quite comprehending what was going on, but being caught up in the atmosphere of joyous celebration.

Being as young as I was at the time amidst what was definitely an adult gathering I felt self-conscious. My brother and sister had pretty much abandoned me at the gate so I just stood in the back and watched as the concert progressed.

One of the things that came out of this time period was the idea that dancing could be done on your own. You could just let your body go to the beat of the music without inhibition. No motion or gyration was considered too weird or bizarre for public display.

As I stood in the back I did tap my foot and occasionally clap my hands to the music but I definitely felt a sense of restraint about how I might look to others if they were to watch me. I don't remember which bands we heard that night except for the last performer: Otis Redding.

There was a delay before Otis Redding came on stage. During this interval quite a few people left. I think many of them must have looked back later and felt like people who leave a baseball game before the end of the ninth inning while their team is many runs behind. The next day they find out that their team rallied in the last inning, won the game and they missed the most exciting part of the whole season. Well that is what happened when Otis Redding finally started to sing.

Otis Redding was a presence on stage that could not be ignored. His intensity and talent were so strong that I found myself swept up into the power of the moment and before I knew it I was out dancing in the aisles with the best of them. No restraint. No inhibitions. Just pure let it all out and move to the music.

That is pretty much how I related to music until I met a different type of musician in 1972, Swami Kriyananda. When I first met Kriyananda I was looking for a place that could support my efforts to learn about and live in harmony with the positive flow of life. I had no idea that music would be a powerful way to attune myself to the positive flow. I thought that music was basically entertainment or at most a way to experience temporary changes in my emotions.

Kriyananda taught me that music is a reflection of the consciousness of the musician. If the music is loud and angry then the composer's consciousness was tapping into loud and angry qualities of consciousness. The musicians playing the music would then tap into and express loud and angry energies while performing the music. The audience would then take in all of that loud and angry energy while listening. Remember how we talked about the ripples when you drop a pebble into water? This is an example of how flows of consciousness move through people and into society at large.

This is not about judgment or telling people that they shouldn't play or listen to loud and angry music or any other style of music. I am using this particular example because it is one of the easiest to see. What we are trying to do is understand clearly what is actually taking place in life. This will give us the information that we need to make conscious choices concerning how we live. Many people do not realize how affected they are by music. If you pay close attention to the effect that different types of music have on your consciousness you will be able to experiment for yourself and see if what I am saying is true.

Some years ago I taught a class for high school students in which we listened to different styles of music while meditating. With our minds and hearts open to the underlying energies of the music we watched to see how we were affected by the music. Invariably the students who were sincerely trying to participate in the experiment could easily tell what qualities of energy were being expressed. Were they joyful, calming and uplifting? Were they neutrally activating? Or were they powerfully activating in a downward-pulling direction?

If you doubt that music has a powerful magnetism to affect people think about the crowds of people at a heavy metal rock concert. Are they filled with vibrations of peace and love? No. Riots, beatings, rapes and even killings are not all that uncommon at such gatherings. Have you ever heard of a killing after a Pavarotti concert? Or a Beach Boys concert?

I am not suggesting that one concert of any type will by itself cause people to act with peak positive or negative energies. People who riot at a rock concert come already primed by the totality of their lives. The group energy of the moment is usually what pushes them over the edge, similar to the way I was moved to dance freely at that Otis Redding concert.

The key here is to realize that we are powerfully affected by the consciousness of the music we listen to. If the music is restless, to the degree of its power and our openness, it will activate restlessness in our consciousness. If the music is blue, we will be blue. If the music is joyful, then we will take joyfulness into our consciousness.

As a society we have become very accepting of a wide variety of musical styles. That openness is expanding and positive, but we also have to be discriminating as individuals.

Sights, Sounds & Inspirations

Just because society allows for all tastes does not mean we have to participate in them all. The real power of living consciously comes when we can make positive choices for ourselves without putting others down for making their choices.

In our efforts to attune ourselves to the positive flow we want to use our formula on the music that we listen to. Observe how you feel during and after any particular song that you hear. Has the music drawn you in an elevating, activating or downward-pulling direction?

If you are not calm enough to tell how you are affected practice meditation to calm your mind. Most people go through life so wound up inside that they can't honestly tell how they feel inside; they only know how they feel on the outside or the periphery of their consciousness.

Another way to go at this is to listen to music that is advertised as calming and uplifting. Even if it seems boring at first, make yourself listen for 15 or 20 minutes. If it puts you to sleep, it was definitely calming. Often people associate calmness with sleep, but if you make a practice of listening to music that is truly calming while at the same time engaging, you will find that it brings you to a relaxed state of greater awareness rather than lowering your energy into sleep.

Keep in mind that the music a very restless person experiences as calming could be very agitating to a person who is firmly rooted in deep calmness. This is an example of the directional nature of our situation. We need to choose things in life that take us from where we are now to where we want to go. In life that is not always a straight line. Sometimes we can make great leaps in our inner growth and at other times we are doing well to take little baby steps. What we want to do is get things moving in the right direction. No matter the size of our steps forward they will all add up to victory in the end as long as we keep moving.

Truly uplifting music will lead us to elevated states of quietness. In the silence of the soul we can hear the mystical symphony of the positive flow. These inner sounds draw us up to ever-higher states of consciousness. This inner realm is where we will find the lasting happiness that we seek.

When you listen to music, practice transmuting the outward vibrations into a greater awareness of your inner connection to the positive flow. Let the sounds come into your heart and then draw that energy up the spine to the spiritual eye. Feel at the spiritual eye that you are releasing that upward flowing energy out into the ocean of life. By connecting everything that we hear to this inner flow we can not only use the sounds that we hear to increase our inner connection, but we can use this inner connection like a lightning rod. Negative energies that flow through us and are dispersed into the ocean of life do not stop in our own consciousness long enough to do us damage.

These same concepts hold true for movies and television. In fact, motion pictures are even more powerful because they include sight as well as sound. Research has shown that visual stimulus along with sound increases memory retention dramatically. So not only are we affected by the movies that we watch, but those effects stay with us much longer than music alone.

Do you know or remember what happened when the movie "The Exorcist" first came out? The experience was so powerful that people in the audience were fainting and throwing up all over the place! I remember going to a horror movie when I was a child. It was about a huge spider that was eating people. I was so scared that I stood in the back of the aisle and peeked around the corner of the doorway! That's pretty powerful stuff.

I also remember going to the movie *The Ten Commandments* at least ten times. I loved that movie. It was thrilling to me that a man could talk with God and that God would show His powers here in this world. While my concepts of God and religion might be different now, the power of the media to uplift is still the same.

100

Sights, Sounds & Inspirations

When we use the tools of any art form to inspire noble qualities in others we are acting as channels for the positive flow. In that process we ourselves receive the blessing of experiencing that positive energy flowing through us. All lives are improved through connection to the positive flow. When we do well for ourselves it benefits everyone we come into contact with.

If we are channels for the negative flow we reap negative rewards. Many of the musicians I once thought inspiring died at early ages from drug and alcohol abuse. As I look back I can see how their music expressed the pain and suffering that they were experiencing. The mixture of energies that came through their music expressed the totality of their consciousness and although it was trying to flow upward, much of it was flowing downward. At the time I thought it was good music. Now I can see that I was not educated enough to know the difference between music that uplifts the soul and music that only stirs up the emotions.

By understanding how these energy flows work and becoming conscious of them we can begin to recognize how they affect us. Just as you wouldn't eat onions if they upset your stomach, you can choose not to attend movies that will upset your inner connection to the positive flow.

Television, movies and music are by definition activating experiences. They can be activating in positive or negative directions but by their nature they stimulate our senses and emotions. When we overexpose ourselves to these stimulants we interfere with the soul's natural state of calmness, thus affecting our ability to perceive the positive flow.

We also set ourselves up for needing ever greater levels of stimulus to feel fully engaged. This is exactly what happens to drug addicts. They need increasing amounts of the drug to feel satisfied. Television, movies, listening to the radio or tapes and CD's - all of these can lead us to a feeling that if we are not being stimulated nothing is happening in our lives. Then we feel bored. When we can't feel the natural joy of life itself flowing through us without outward stimulus we have definitely disconnected from the positive flow.

Many people do not realize how noise pollution affects their peace of mind. One of the most powerful ways to understand and reverse the effects of constant listening and talking is to spend some time in silence. Take a day or more and simply do not talk. Don't watch television or listen to music. Wear earplugs if there is a lot of noise in the surrounding environment. Read an uplifting book, write, attend to a hobby or anything else that is not overly stimulating, but do not talk or listen unnecessarily. If it is not possible to do this at home then go to a retreat or out into nature where you can walk without being disturbed.

At first it may seem strange, but soon you will find silence to be a wonderful haven of peace. When re-entering society's stimulations you will be amazed at how much is going on that you did not notice before. This greater awareness of what is going on around you and its effect on your consciousness will be invaluable for developing your inner attunement to the positive flow.

I am not saying that we should never listen to music, go to the movies or watch television. Nor am I suggesting that we should pompously point our noses up in the air and think, "I only ingest the purest forms of art that are untainted by any tinges of the negative flow!" - which is almost impossible since there are so few. What we are aiming to do is manage these stimulants in the same way we manage our diet. Be aware of the qualities of energy that you are taking in. Choose a simple diet of these types of stimulants and then refine your choices as your sensitivities guide you.

Here's a guideline for evaluating music: Elevating music draws us toward a dynamic state of inner stillness while activating music brings us out of stillness toward outward restlessness and fluctuating emotions. Downward-pulling music stimulates negative emotions.

Sights, Sounds & Inspirations

In the beginning you may experience some mental upheaval as the result of withdrawing from the aural and visual stimulants that your mind has become used to. It is the same as getting off any other kind of addiction. Distract yourself from these symptoms by engaging in positively charged activities that are elevating. Don't confuse the symptoms of withdrawal with the idea that you are less fulfilled as the result of those stimulants not being in your life.

Remember, we are talking about how we can be happy in life - not the temporary enjoyment that comes from an hour or two of having a "good time" but the kind of happiness that is unaffected by good times or bad. Our attunement to the positive flow will connect us to an inner well-spring of happiness which is our release from the ups and downs of desires into the ocean of ever-new joy.

Chapter 15
Working with Your Life

Do you need to find a job? Re-evaluate your current position or direction? Decide what you should "really" be doing with your life? Choose a new location for your home or business? Come up with creative advertising copy or fresh ways of displaying your products? Get along better with co-workers or your boss? Instill positive work ethics in yourself or others? The positive flow is the source of solutions to every challenge in life and we carry it within ourselves all of the time - we simply need to use it.

You see, living in the positive flow of life isn't only about feeling good inside. It is also about expressing that good feeling outwardly in practical ways. As positive energies flow through us we uplift ourselves while simultaneously acting as channels for positive consciousness to flow into this world and help others.

As we develop our ability to observe life clearly and attune ourselves to positive ideas we will find that we can use this ability in everything that we do.

The process of working with our lives while staying inwardly connected to the positive flow is both a science and an art. The techniques of meditation and the principles of how to live in harmony with life are the same for everyone but how we manifest these truths is individual.

Working with Your Life

Let me share some stories about how these ideas have been made real in my life. Use these examples to get a feel for how you can work with these ideas in your own life. Since we are talking about working with our lives, let's use the workplace as our laboratory to explore these principles. Keep in mind that while I am focusing on issues surrounding the workplace, the same concepts can be applied to all areas of life.

In 1978 I was living in Sacramento, California, helping to establish a new branch of a spiritual organization with which I am affiliated. The group was very small. At first my co-founder and I decided that we would not work outside but trust that the income from classes and Sunday donations would suffice. For a number of months we managed to survive.

One day we decided to reconsider our choice. We meditated on the issue and sought inner guidance. We both felt that it was time to work outside for more income. Since one of my skills was that of a piano technician I decided to apply for a position in a piano store. I made a list of stores from the phone book but did not need the whole list because the first place I went into hired me! They had recently lost a salesman and were about to start seeking a new one.

Coincidence you might say?

In 1985 I was living with my family in Santa Barbara, California. I had been working as a photocopier salesman for about six months. Things were going well for me; I even won a sales contest and a free trip to the Caribbean. Upon returning from the trip I was to be promoted to manager of a new branch office. Right before leaving on the trip I discovered that my supervisor lied to me about certain ways the company was to operate. Subsequently while on the trip to the beautiful Island of St. Martin I realized that I couldn't work for them anymore.

When I returned home I gave notice. I had no idea what I would do next to support my family. During my last two weeks as a copier salesman I inwardly opened myself up to ideas about what I should do. One day I remembered my experience getting the piano sales job in Sacramento. At first I thought it was just a pleasant memory; but it persisted. As I explored the memory I inwardly felt a surge of enthusiasm and positive energy going up my spine, so even though they say lightning doesn't strike twice in the same place, since the music store idea had worked before, why not again?

The next day I walked into a music store that sold not only pianos but almost every other type of instrument as well. At the front counter I asked to speak with the owner and was directed to a man sitting at a desk in the back of the store. He was on the phone so I politely kept my distance. When he finished his conversation I approached and introduced myself. I explained that I was looking for a job. He asked about my qualifications. We spoke for about 40 minutes.

By the end of our conversation he was just shaking his head back and forth with a smile on his face. "You have no idea!" he said. "That call I just placed was for an ad that I was about to run in the newspaper. I was going to advertise for a sales position seeking someone with a background just like yours!"

Not only did I get the job but I received invaluable training that led me to owning my own music store in a different city just six months later! I could never have scripted the events that took place, but because I consciously entered into the flow and trusted that things would work out, they did.

Still think it is a coincidence?

Some years ago I experienced a gradual lessening of my income. At first I didn't pay much attention to it. Cycles of greater or lesser financial success are like the tides in the ocean. These ebbs and flows are natural and not something to be all that concerned with. During this time in my life I began to realize that doorways of opportunity in all areas of my life and the surrounding community seemed to be closing before my eyes for no apparent reason. At first it was so gradual that I didn't notice it. When I finally did take a good hard look at how things were going I found there was a pattern that was increasing its power in my life. It wasn't a negative experience. No one was mad at me. It was more like an energy of closure. It was like my job there was finished and it was time to move on.

The energy in our lives has a certain momentum and often, even when we realize that changes need to be made, we can't seem to get off the train of our current circumstances long enough to get a perspective on what is happening. At first I thought I would just go out and get a part time job to supplement my income. I fully expected to get hired at the first place I went. It had always worked for me in the past. This wasn't going to be any big deal.

Well, not only did the first place not hire me, but neither did the second, third, fourth, fifth and so on past twenty. I cannot tell you how surprised I was. This had never happened to me!

I suppose the potentially embarrassing thing about this is that it took me so long to figure out what was really going on. It wasn't until I was turned down for a job delivering pizza that the light started to shine somewhere inside of me.

I mean, here I was with years of workplace experience and I got turned down for a pizza delivery job! I was shocked. I couldn't believe it. I looked the owner of the store right in the eye and asked, "You are turning me down for a delivery position?"

He said, with total equanimity, "Yes."

My ensuing laughter may have reinforced his decision but I couldn't help myself. I realized that life had been having a little fun with me. Remember when I mentioned that the positive flow is conscious and that it has a sense of humor? Well, that conscious power of good in my life was playing a joke on me and I had to admit it was pretty funny.

All I had to do now was work the formula. So here is what I did.

This whole process of job rejections and community door closing was about my needing to observe that it was a time for change in my life. We are all receiving direction from the positive flow daily. The fact that we do not always recognize this subtle information does not mean that it is not there. Now that I had finally gotten the message it was time to attune to a solution. So I started consciously opening myself up to new inspirations from the positive flow about what to do.

During this time of conscious inward openness I was scheduled to visit my sister in Santa Cruz, California. As soon as I arrived the idea of an experiment popped into my mind. What would it be like if I moved to Santa Cruz?

Over the next three days I mentally went through the process of moving to Santa Cruz. I looked up ads for a place to live and found several that seemed likely possibilities. I spent some time trying to imagine how it would feel to live in them. I asked myself, "What would my life be like here?" At the same time I kept my inner connection to Spirit open and asked, "Is this what I should do?"

Then I decided that the real test would be if I could get a job. Would the doors open for me? Or would they still be closed like they had been at home? For a moment I wondered if there was a dark cloud following me. But I knew better than to let that kind of negative thought take root in my mind so I strengthened my resolve to move forward with positive energy.

The negative flow often tries to thwart us when we start off in new positive directions. Self-doubt is one of the ways our good energy can be undermined. Guidance from the positive flow never manifests within us as negative energy. The negative energies of life outside may be a signal that we need to make a change, but the inner guidance to do so will always be felt as a positive energy.

I checked the classified ads again and came up with several job possibilities. I called the one that seemed most interesting and made an appointment for an interview the next day. After chatting with the owners of the business for about half an hour they offered me the position. I couldn't help smiling, but this time it was because the doors were open again. To add to the humor of the situation, it was another delivery position - cake instead of pizza - at a substantially higher pay rate as well!

I told the owners of the business that I would call them the next day with my decision. That night I really searched deeply within myself to feel guidance from the positive flow. I had started the experiment as just that, an experiment. It was more for exploration and entertainment than a serious desire to move specifically to Santa Cruz. What was I supposed to do now?

This had become a classic situation in working with the positive flow. Once we receive inspirations and move in new directions we can become so excited with the opening up of new doorways of opportunity that we lose our higher sense of direction. I could easily have taken the job offer as a sign to make the move and signed up for the job on the spot. What if they gave the job to someone else while I was thinking about it? What if this, what if that?

Here is a key point: The restless mind worries about what can go wrong in life. The calm mind feels at rest and doesn't over-react to life's challenges.

That night as I sat in the silence after meditation it became clear to me that the lesson of the moment was the willingness to move; the willingness to look at possibilities beyond the spectrum of previously considered solutions. I realized I was supposed to push forward with my life, but Santa Cruz was only one possibility. Next I would need to open myself up to other possibilities as well.

The answer about where to go did not come to me right away. I held myself open to absolutely any location. I was willing to move literally anywhere in the world that I inwardly felt would be right. I kept myself inwardly connected and added patience to my efforts.

Since I did not yet have an answer and my finances were becoming somewhat dire, I decided to get a newspaper and look in the ads again. Sometimes when the energy isn't flowing, doing anything is better than standing still. A little positive energy applied in practical directions can often prime the pump for larger changes.

Strangely, my local store was out of newspapers, so I drove to another store several miles away. They were out of papers as well. I thought, "What's this all about?" That night I received a totally unexpected call with a job offer. Less then a month later I had moved to a new town and found that once again all of the doors in my life were open.

It is essential during this whole process to stay keenly observant of what is going on in your life. Seek the energies underneath the outward circumstances. Then attune to creative solutions and experiment.

Even if your efforts do not seem to be working several very important things will be happening for you. The first is that by maintaining your inner connection to the positive flow you will remain positive during a difficult situation. That by itself is a very valuable result. The second thing is that you will be creating a positive magnetism which will draw a positive resolution to the situation. Regardless of whether the solution is one that comes through your inner inspiration or spontaneously presents itself from the outside, your efforts will have helped to draw the desired result.

This is one of the most powerful results of living in the positive flow. Somehow, through the magic of life itself, the things that we need in our lives will come to us and present themselves. All we need to do is put out positive energies and stay awake and aware enough - inwardly and outwardly - to realize what is trying to happen in our lives.

The real solution to my situation was not "to move or not to move," it was in working consciously and dynamically with the positive flow. Maybe my life would have been even better if I had moved to Santa Cruz. Maybe if I had just persisted where I was living things would have worked out there just as well.

Remember, there is not just one way that truth can manifest and we are never abandoned no matter what choices we make in life.

Just so I don't leave you in suspense...I should mention that the move ended up being extremely benefical both spiritually and monetarily.

The most thrilling stories in history are filled with examples of people who followed the light of their inner inspirations. While it is true that not all of our dreams will materialize as expected; to live without the courage of our convictions is to not fully live, but to just exist.

This same process of inner attunement can give you specific solutions or draw positive resolutions to every aspect of your daily adventure in life. So have fun with it and realize that the real work that we do in life is on ourselves rather than the job that we go to in order to support ourselves financially.

The idea that our work in this life is more about who we are on the inside than what we do on the outside is a very important one. Many people sacrifice the quality and integrity of their inner being in order to manifest material success for their outer being. We all know the ways, some large and some small, that we have compromised our principles for some short term gain. Let us dedicate ourselves ever more fully to expressing in our outward actions, our inward resolve to express only qualities of the positive flow.

Chapter 16
Flowing with Relationships

Have you ever wondered why the saints are so magnetic? Why thousands of people flock to be near them? This overpowering presence of love is the greatest magnetic force in the universe. When each of us in our own way channels this loving presence into the world we are expressing and increasing our connection to the positive flow.

This approach to life is so eminently practical that it fits into literally every nook and cranny of our lives. You will note that all of the suggestions that I make cover points that are universally applicable to all situations. Mixing and matching the correct blend to your individual situation is your part of applying the art of living in the positive flow. Remember, the idea is to observe your inner oneness with all people. Attune to inspirations for how you can serve and please them. Then experiment with the creative ideas that come to you.

Keep in mind that success in this process is not limited to whether the focus of your attention responds in the way that you hope. As the saying goes: You can lead a horse to water but you cannot make the horse drink. Nor should you try to make others respond to your good intentions. Part of the process is to respect the freedom of others to be the way they want to be. If that shuts you out in some way, do not let hurt feelings get in the way of gracefully accepting their choices.

Flowing with Relationships

You will notice that I mentioned trying to please people as a part of serving them. This has to do with tuning in to their preferences. It does not mean that we should give up our principles. As often as possible we should try to help people in ways that are pleasing to them; like sugaring the lemonade to their taste, letting them choose a restaurant or movie or trying not to clutter up their home with our stuff when we visit them. When we take the time and effort to reach out to others in pleasing ways we are giving power to our caring, expanding positive energies through our lives into the world and growing beyond selfish ego identification.

Try to anticipate the little ways that you can be kind to everyone you meet. Dale Carnegie in his book *How to Win Friends and Influence People* suggested that this could be as simple as complementing a person on the color of their hair. The key is to stay attentive for opportunities to share positive energy with others. When we busy our minds by expanding into other people's realities we loosen our identification with our own ego. This is one of the great powers of selfless service.

This practice also opens us up to meeting new people and being entertained or inspired in unexpected ways. Life is rich with untapped possibilities. Let's not cut ourselves off from them because of fear of offending or involving ourselves in the lives of others.

Parental relationships are a tough area for many people. For those who have a naturally positive relationship with their parents: thank your lucky stars! At the same time, for those that have a rough relationship with their parents, you can thank your lucky stars as well. The incredible thing about life is that we have been magnetically drawn to the precise situations that we need in order to grow spiritually. No matter what the particulars of your parental relationships, there are lessons to be learned.

Remember to observe.

My father and I never got along in this life. We sometimes went years without talking because every time we talked there was an argument. It took me a long time to realize that the very things which drove me away from him were his greatest blessings to me.

My father's basic philosophy about life was that you should make all the money that you can and store it away where thieves can't get it. Making money was his religion. He was good at it. He made a lot of money. He was also one of the most unhappy people I have ever known.

Since my teenage years I have rejected that philosophy. It wasn't hard for me to do since I could see that having lots of money did not make people happy. I spent many years of my youth yearning for happiness. Now, all these years later, I can see that my father's caustic nature was part of what compelled me to seek my own answers about life. If he had drawn me in with a more benevolent nature I might never have sought so earnestly to find the deeper truths about life.

Of course, I could also have made the choice to be just like my father in spite of my dislike for his choices. Or I could have hated him for not nurturing me as a child. But I realized that by hating him I would be carrying the energy of hate. Why should I let his choices in life poison the peace of my life? I decided to love him instead. That way at least one of us could be happy!

The key here is to understand that we have lessons to be learned from the families into which we are born. Sometimes the lesson is to get out of town fast! For some it is simply to appreciate the blessings of a truly loving and harmonious family. For most people it is somewhere between those two extremes. What we want to do is seek ways that transmute the energies of our family relationships into qualities that represent ever-greater expressions of the positive flow.

If you are a parent, then you know how challenging the process of raising and then releasing a child into the world can be. For those who have not experienced the joys of parenting, all I can say is that if you really want to test your internal metal in the fires of selfless service then sign up for parenting. Talk about adventures!

The subject of parenting is so vast that I have dedicated two separate books to the subject. The first is entitled *Doorway to a New Lifetime: Childbirth from a Spiritual View.* In this book I talk about using these principles in every part of the childbirth process: starting before conception through the actual birth and even some thoughts on choosing a name. In my next book, *Positive Flow Parenting* I go into detail about using the *Way of the Positive Flow* for all stages of parenting, including some thoughts on how to relate to your children once they have grown up.

Having mentioned these books there are a couple of points that I would like to include here.

In the beginning of this book I made it clear that we are discussing a process that we can apply to literally every life experience. Parenting is no exception. The *Way of the Positive Flow* not only provides the process whereby we can be good parents, but if we communicate to our children how this works while we are raising them it will become a natural part of the way that they relate to the world. Isn't one of the main goals of parenting to give our children the tools through which they can live successful lives? What greater gift could we pass on to our children then knowledge about how life itself works and how each of us can tune in to and utilize this understanding to benefit ourselves and others? This is essential information that should be at the foundation of a good education.

My final thought on parenting for this book is that our children are not "ours". Parents do not own their children. No matter how much love, sweat and tears we expend to help them towards adulthood it is essential that we see our efforts as expressions of selfless service. There are few greater tests for a parent than that we should offer ourselves to our children without obligation of return. I don't mean that they shouldn't express appreciation, they should, but it should be expressed

Way of the Positive Flow

because they want to express it, not because we demand that they do.

Let us not make slaves of our children. Love them, nurture them and then release them to their adventures in living. This attitude will not only free parents from negative attachments and the chains of obligation that many parents use to pressure their grown offspring, but it will honor and respect the divine spark that radiates independently in all souls.

In fact, this is a good basis for all relationships!

When we use our relationships with others to improve ourselves and help others we are taking advantage of one of life's greatest opportunities for personal growth. If you are with someone and you feel any kind of disharmony, practice our formula and consciously bring the positive flow into the mix. With those that you feel a natural harmony, use the positive flow to raise the quality of that relationship from beautiful to divine. Through attunement to the positive flow we can break the boundaries of human separateness and see all of life as an expression of the one Infinite Spirit.

Chapter 17
Three Pervasive Challenges

Rooted deep in the recesses of the way we are made there are impulses that drive our lives. Like weather patterns around the world or the cycles of time that control the movement of solar systems and universes, so it is that there are forces at work underneath the specifics of our individual lives. The energies of love, peace and joy are examples of the positive powers that move us toward an ever-expanding awareness of life and its potential. Three of the most pervasive ways that the negative flow can keep us bound to the finite creation are through the powers of intoxicants, sexuality and greed.

With the mapping of the human DNA genome some scientists believe they will be able to account for the reasons that some people are predisposed to alcoholism and drug addiction. They also hope to find gene markers that will account for sexual drive, worldly ambition and any number of other powerful forces that seem to take hold over the lives of people.

In the beginning of our discussion we talked about how scientists look at life from the outside in and saints look at life from the inside out. When considering these opposing perspectives it is easy to get the impression that the exploration of truth is dependent on one view or the other. You are either a saint or an unbelieving scientific sinner! This is the common stance that many take in life - truth is either this or

117

that. The reality is that life is an amazing multi-layered web of interconnected levels of understanding that can be explored inwardly and outwardly.

As souls, we have been born into physical forms that have great power over our experience in this world. To deny the influence of heredity is a very limiting point of view. It is also very limiting to think of ourselves as bound and controlled solely by our genetic history.

Underneath the influence of genetics are the founding forces of life itself. These forces can be aligned with the positive flow expanding towards infinity or they can be expressions of the negative flow leading towards limitation and the dual pleasure/pain nature of this world.

Remember, the responsibility of the negative flow is to keep the creation going. How can something finite keep us from seeking that which is infinite? By creating the illusion that happiness in life can be found through the senses and the emotions. The negative flow powers this false impression with rewards of temporary pleasures that glimmer with sparkles of good feeling while they distract us from their hidden underbelly of disappointment.

Let's use these three over arching areas - intoxicants, sexuality and greed - to see how this works.

Intoxicants

Many people think that the most basic of human instincts is self-preservation. Yet if you consider the large number of suicides and noble offerings of one life for another, there seems to be an even stronger force at work. That force is the simple desire to be happy. Each soul is born from an infinite sea of ever-new joy and deep within each of us is a memory of that reality. We can never be completely fulfilled until we return to that joy.

Everything that we do in life can be traced back to our desire to be happy. Unfortunately, we keep looking outside ourselves for that fulfillment. Lasting happiness slips ever just beyond our grasp. This constant struggle causes us discomfort so, to dim the frustration, many seek to drown their sorrows in their preferred form of indulgence.

At first the indulgence in alcohol or drugs may seem just an innocent jaunt into the frivolity of life. Let us live life to the fullest and party while we can! But as with all outward experiences after the high there is always a balancing low; if a person was already unhappy when they started indulging, the low afterward can be devastating. Thus it is that people get swept up into the cycle of ups and downs that become the lifestyle of the addicted.

Scientists expect to explain alcoholism and drug addiction by finding the genes that are responsible for these problems. It is not uncommon for people to describe these as diseases. In a way, people who suffer from these life challenges are being told, "It is not your fault, it is a disease and we will try to find a cure for you. Just wait and do your best while we figure this out." The truth is that we are born into bodies that are magnetically in tune with our predisposition of consciousness. So if we have not yet conquered the temptation to try to intoxicate our way to happiness we will be born into a body that is aligned with this challenge.

Please do not think that I am suggesting we let those addicted to drugs or alcohol wallow in their own mire. I'm just pointing out that true healing comes from self-acceptance, taking responsibility for our current circumstances and the will to improve things in the future. Once a soul has come to that understanding then help can actually help.

Does this mean that every drink, puff or sniff is inherently evil? No. But it does mean that we are playing with fire. We do not consciously know what our karmic history is. For some, it will take only one drink or puff in this lifetime to reactivate a problem from the past.

It is helpful to remember that the temptation to indulge in these things is powered by a magnetic force that comes

119

directly from the negative flow. It is like getting too close to a powerful river in flood. If you are not careful you can be swept in beyond your ability to help yourself.

Keep in mind, anything that tries to impose itself on our free will is not our friend. Addicting substances usurp our free will. They take control of us and limit our ability to act successfully in this world. Even more importantly, they limit our ability to perceive and grow in our relationship with the positive flow. The best way to strengthen ourselves against these addicting forces is to immerse our consciousness in the inner joy of the positive flow. Once the soul has drunk deeply from the ocean of Spirit, temporary outward stimulants will lose their false luster and their power to bind us.

Does this mean that occasional indulgence in these things is bad? What about Italians who drink wine with their meals the way many people drink water?

The avoidance of intoxicants is certainly the safest path. Even so, many people will experiment to find out for themselves.

Remember, the bar (pun intended!) for evaluating these things is: How does it effect my ability to feel connected to the positive flow?

Both alcohol and drugs cause the user to be tied more firmly to body consciousness. You can see this in the lifestyles that usually accompany their use.

I should mention that recreational drugs have a greater negative effect on the ability of the mind to achieve calmness then light alcohol use. But in either case, the issue isn't about good or bad; it is about our commitment to living on a higher level.

In the end it is up to you to evaluate how these things affect you. Through honest introspection you will be able to make a conscious choice instead of just going along with the crowd. Do not relate to this subject passively. Intoxicants are very much like fire: they can be beautiful in one moment and burn you the next. Don't be mesmerized by the flame of "good times". So…imbibe with caution. Instead, intoxicate yourself with the joy of Spirit.

Sexuality

We discussed our dilemma with the senses and sensuality in chapter eight. I have discussed sexuality at length in my book *Doorway to a New Lifetime: Childbirth from a Spiritual View*. So let me start this section by saying that there is much more that can be said.

Sex is a lot like riding a roller coaster (I'm not referring to the physical act!). Finding a partner is like waiting in line. It could be a short line or a long line. Generally speaking, the longer the line the greater the anticipation. The first hill is foreplay: the longer the foreplay the higher the ride. Orgasm is the thrilling plunge down the highest hill, followed up by various less intense - though pleasurable - thrashing about. Finally the end of the ride comes and you either get off or you go again for another round. (Ah, youth!)

The physical union of two loving souls can be one of the most beautiful experiences in this world. There is nothing unclean or evil about it. We just need to remember that all experiences in this world are temporary and limited. That is the nature of this world. To truly and ultimately become one with another being we must merge our individual natures into the oneness of Spirit. So as close as we might feel to our partner, the truth is that we cannot merge physically, only spiritually.

I know it is disappointing. Our hearts yern to melt into our loved ones in the same way that we release in orgasm. We instinctively know that merging is possible. And we are right, it is! It just cannot be done physically or emotionally. This is another example of the insidious way the negative flow fools us into acting in ways that do not lead to the promised reward. Sex brings us right to the threshold of glory and then it yanks us back. Not knowing that we have an alternative, we accept occasional glimpses of paradise as being all we can achieve.

Way of the Positive Flow

Because this glimpse is so powerful many seek to break through by repeatedly knocking at the door. Some seek union with partners that they have no love relationship with. These efforts inevitably lead to a lessening of enjoyment, as well as a hardening of the heart. When sex is turned toward self-indulgence rather than an expansion of love, it is turned towards the negative flow.

Remember, life is directional. Ask yourself: Which way am I going? Is my sexuality expanding my heart and positive life qualities? Or is it making me smaller by immersing me in overindulgence of the senses and a preoccupation with my own desires? Most of us know the answers to these questions. The larger issue is what we do with that knowledge. Do we control our desires or do they control us?

Another aspect of sexuality is its connection to our emotions. The tendency for most people is to think that love is rooted in emotions rather than universal love. When we love someone with our emotions we are subject to the ups and downs of our personal preferences.

There are countless romance novels where intense love is expressed with great fanfare and then in the next chapter that "endless love" is turned into hate. How can a person say, "I love you" in one moment and "I hate you" in the next? Because they are not in love, they are in emotion. If we say we love someone and they leave us for another, so then we hate them; we only loved with our emotions. Our emotionally based love was subject to the preference that this person not leave us for another.

True love is a feeling rooted in the universal ocean of love. When you truly love someone, you will let them go to seek their own truth. Love never binds. It is never withdrawn. When you love someone you may not agree with their choices, but you do not withdraw your love because of those choices. All too many couples start with what they think is perfect love and end up going to war across the table of divorce.

Three Pervasive Challenges

Love/hate relationships should really be called like/ dislike relationships. These are emotion-based feelings that swing with our personal view of the way things should be. The feelings of the positive flow are not emotion-based. They do not have the duality of ups and downs. When we root our feelings in the positive flow they will not fluctuate like emotions.

Strong emotions are often in play before, during and after sex. Couples often have arguments before or after sex and sometimes even while they are doing it! It is important to understand that if we allow our emotions to swing wildly in one direction, they will inevitable turn back and swing an equal distance in the opposite direction. Make up sex after an argument is not love, it is emotion. That is why we should seek equanimity in our lives through even-mindedness.

In the midst of all life experiences we want to stay connected to the positive flow and keep our energy flowing in towards the spine and up through the heart to the spiritual eye. When we keep this inner connection strong, we are much less likely to be ambushed by wayward emotions.

The power of sexuality is rooted in the energy centers of the spine. Energy rising from the base of the spine up towards the brain powers our spiritual transformation from finite to infinite awareness. So our sexual energy can actually help us spiritually. The issue is whether it takes us down and out through the senses or inward and upward to strengthen our inner connection to Spirit.

As with all intoxicants - sexual energy is certainly a strong one - be cautious. Use our formula. Observe your sexual energies. Seek inspiration in working with those energies. Experiment with ways that you can use these forces to power your inner quest for truth.

Greed

It is said in some circles that making big money is better than sex. You do not have to be a millionaire to experience the surge of energy that comes with making what to you is a big deal, getting a raise or coming into unexpected wealth. You are riding high! You are on a roll! "Nothing can hold me back now, baby!" Hmm. Pretty strong emotions aren't they?

How about gamblers? They know all about the ups and downs of life. The surge of energy that comes with winning is just as addictive as chemical drugs.

The desire for money is more often than not an expression of the underlying desire for power. The ego wants power over life. The ego wants to control, not to be controlled. The ego wants what it wants, when it wants it. And as the golden rule is sometimes explained: He who has the gold, rules.

So the ego makes the classic assumption of the negative flow: the more I have of money, the happier I will be. It is this fallacious idea that causes untold miseries in this world. Seekers of the great god Money always find in the end that money does not equal happiness. Unfortunately, in their quest for money they are almost always willing to trample others in order to get it. Their personal greed overcomes all sense of propriety and they sow a negative flow of energy for themselves and many others.

The urge for personal power can be used for good or ill. When it feeds the ego it turns towards the negative flow, self-aggrandizement and suffering. As we know, egos can get pretty big, but they are always subject to the limitations of the physical world, they always eventually pop. When turned towards the positive flow the urge for success brings freedom from the ego by providing the drive that leads to self-improvement. When we are fully identified with Infinite Spirit the power of the universe is ours to express. This is the real underlying source of all success in life, inwardly and outwardly.

So, as always, the negative flow promises greatness and delivers disappointment. Through the positive flow, as the negative side of the ego becomes weaker, our Spirit grows towards infinite strength and we can accomplish literally anything that is ours to accomplish.

Three Pervasive Challenges

Just as the poisoning and healing herbs of the forest lay side by side, so do the positive and negative polarities of consciousness live side by side. At the center of every life experience is an opportunity to grow towards the light of Spirit, or to turn away from the light into the darkness of limitation. This is the threshold where we experience success or failure in life. These are the true milestones by which our lives are measured. Let us seek to avoid all things that limit our ability to grow in Spirit. And when limiting energies of this world cannot be avoided, let us turn the tide by offering them inwardly to the positive flow.

No challenge is too great in life. We are never tested beyond our ability to succeed. The key is to realize that success in life has much less to do with outward success than with an indomitable Spirit. Grow your spirit strong and all outward successes will follow.

Chapter 18
Dealing with Emotions

My mother told me a story that took place during my childhood that will help us begin our discussion about emotions. I have no recollection of this story, but I have no doubt that it is true.

When I was four years old my mother took me grocery shopping at a local market. As we were walking down one of the aisles a product apparently caught my eye and I decided that I wanted it. In the time honored fashion of parent/child relationships, my mother said, "No." I said, "I want it!"

As our tug of war escalated my mother could see that I was winding up for a big one. She definitely didn't want to give in and neither did I. When I played my biggest card she also pulled out hers.

Young children do not have a great many tools in their arsenal for getting their own way. In my search for success I tossed caution to the wind. I threw myself down onto the floor and while wildly kicking my feet and tossing my arms about I yelled at the top of my lungs, "I want it! I want it! I want it!"

My mother's solution to the situation was truly powerful. She simply walked away and out of the store without me. She took up a station outside where she could see through the window that I was safe. Then she just waited.

Dealing with Emotions

At first I was so caught up in my bellowing I didn't notice her absence. Eventually realizing my audience was gone I gradually settled down. Once I was calmer I found that I was alone in the store without my mother. By the time I found her outside I was so happy to see her that I forgot all about whatever it was that started the whole affair.

The exaggerated emotional responses that children express are at times comical. At the time I am sure that I felt the fate of the world was dependent on the fulfillment of my desire. Now I can look back and laugh at how silly I was at the time. Can you imagine an adult having a tantrum like that in the aisle of a store? Yet, if we think about it, we have all seen or been the recipient of an emotional outburst by an "adult" that is basically the same as my childish outburst in that store. You may even have had an outburst like this yourself.

We are going to come back to this little story so it can help us to understand some of the dynamics of our emotions and how we can work with them. But first, we need to have a better feel for the source of our emotions and how they can help or hinder us in our quest for happiness. Just like the motor in a car, our mind and emotions are part of a larger mechanism. Let's take a moment to look at some of the overarching systems.

The mind is the foundation of our current mental capacity. Its ability to perceive is not in any way affected by what it perceives. It simply registers perception. The mind sees a horse, a tree or a dog. The mind doesn't label them as such or have any feelings about them, it just registers a perception. Like a mirror, the mind simply reflects that which is before it.

The intellect is the file keeper of mental perception. It categorizes and gives definition to that which we perceive. That is a horse, a tree, a dog. The intellect has no reaction to that which it sees.

The ego is the soul identified with the body. This is where we create identifications like your horse, a tree in the forest, my dog. This process of identification helps us to function

127

in this world; it is a necessary part of the whole. The negative side of the ego is that it identifies us with limited territories in life. I am this body/mind. I am not that tree. That dog is separate from me. To function in this world that is helpful information, but it hides the underlying reality that all of life is one. The ego takes us away from universal identification and ties us to a specific smaller portion of the whole.

The ego alone is not the real difficulty with our current circumstances. The real culprit is feeling. Feelings are the qualities of energy that say, "I like the tree, I don't like the horse." And even more importantly, "That is my dog, I like my dog, don't mess with my dog or I will mess with you!"

Feelings are our likes and dislikes in life. They result from a complex union of energies that determine our current state of consciousness. On the outside they come from a combination of our genetics and our reaction to the environment we have experienced up to this point in life. On the inside they come from a combination of our past lives and the qualities of energy that we have been putting out in this life. These energies from the past have drawn us to our current life circumstances. They drive our underlying urges. The choices that we make today determine what we are sowing for the future.

Like a costume or the body of a car, our bodies and personalities cover these inner workings of mind, intellect, ego and feelings. This combined whole is what we have learned to accept as a definition of who we are.

The physical bodies that our souls are animating with consciousness come in different sizes and shapes. They are like the instruments of an orchestra. They can be played with focused accomplishment creating a well rounded tone or they can be poorly played creating screeching sounds of all kinds. Some bodies are beautiful to look at on the outside but flawed on the inside. A good sounding instrument can be sturdy and at other times frail. Sometimes instruments get out of tune, broken or have parts that wear out and need replacing. Any number of combinations of these different qualities makes up the wide diversity of body/mind combinations that we call humankind.

Our emotions are reflections of our inner likes and dislikes. They are the manifestations of how our personalities feel about things. It is important to remember that as souls we are not our personalities. The personality is just a temporary covering through which we live this life. The qualities of energy that animate the personality are what we carry from lifetime to lifetime.

So…what is the practical purpose of all this esoteric wandering?

Just this: When we live through fluctuating emotions, we can never be truly happy. Our joy, peace and overall sense of well-being will always be subject to things outside of ourselves. We will only be happy when life gives us what we want. When we do not get what we want we will feel a sense of lack and/or disappointment. Of course these kinds of feelings can spur us on to achieve positive goals in this life. That is helpful. When the friction of life causes us to seek inner improvement it is our friend. But when it drives us into thinking that more things or a higher paying job will give us happiness, it digs us into a deeper hole.

Let's go back to the story at the beginning of this chapter and see what we can learn in the light of these underlying energies that we have been talking about.

First of all, we can see that I was only four years old and very immature. Of course, I have also met eighty year olds that are very immature. This is not as much an issue of years, but of understanding and self-control. Maturity brings the ability to stand aside from our personal preferences and discern truth or that which is most beneficial at any given time. Wild emotions keep us from feeling peace and without peace we cannot hear the inner voice of truth.

This is why stress and restlessness are so rampant in our society. People live in their senses causing ripples of restlessness

Way of the Positive Flow

in the mind which inevitably stir up emotional responses. If the mind is kept calm, it will not be drawn into the ups and downs of the emotions.

Some might think that this idea represents a state of negative emptiness. What will I be without my feelings? What I am suggesting is that we replace immature emotional responses to life with a deep connection to life's underlying ocean of peace. People who have never experienced a dynamic state of inner peace may have trouble grasping what this means and how it works. This inner state of consciousness provides the strength and equanimity that we need in order to rise beyond the ups and downs of life. When we feel connected to this inner sense of well-being we will never want to lose it. Strong emotions of either happy/sad or like/dislike can disconnect us; not because emotions are bad, but because the fluctuating energies that they cause in the mind create restlessness. The waters of the mind cannot be calm and agitated at the same time.

The solution to dealing with strong emotions is not to suppress them. We are not seeking to hide our dirt under the rug. If we try to deal with emotions that way they will eventually spill out and make an even bigger mess. What we want to do is redirect that energy in positive directions. Use it to raise your level of consciousness. Draw your strong feelings into the spine and focus them up at the spiritual eye. Take slow deep breaths in the nose and out the mouth. After a few deep breaths, send a beacon of your rising energies out into the universe. Feel that you are releasing all tension and personal desire. Let yourself be emptied of agitation. Then feel from the center of your heart an artesian well of peace opening up and filling your whole being.

This might sound like a bunch of hocus pocus, up in the air space talk to those who have never tried it, but I can tell you from personal experience it has worked for thousands of people, including myself. Maybe it will work for you!

Arguing about how things should be is pretty typical of human interactions at all ages. People are constantly verbally or physically poking at each other. Not only does this cause us to lose our own peace, but it can cause others to lose their peace as well. Certainly they have the choice about how to react to our energies, but when we put out negative energies we cause others to be put in the position of needing to choose. So that attaches consequences to us.

Another aspect of this is that we cannot truly hear what others feel or think about things when our emotions are whipped up into a frenzy. The mind can't register a clear understanding of the views of others through the fog of emotional turmoil. Thus, it is essential for people to be calm when they communicate.

Here is a guiding principle: Reason tends to follow feeling.

No matter how we feel, we can always find reasons to support our feelings. And in fact, the reasoning that supports our feelings will almost always come up first and most powerfully in our mind. So we cannot trust our reasoning when the mind is clouded with strong emotions.

The key here is to always live connected to the positive flow within us. When we are inwardly connected we feel in balance. Life's variety of circumstances won't easily be able to knock us around. When new sailors go out to sea they have trouble keeping their footing in the rolling waves. Experienced sailors can keep their balance even in a big storm. So it is with our practice of living centered in the positive flow. In the beginning we find ourselves affected by the little ups and downs of the emotions. With practice we will find that there is a great strength of peace and joy inside of ourselves that can carry us through any storm that life may bring us.

Another thing that we can learn from our story is that negative energies need our attention to have power over us. When we withdraw our attention they almost always disappear. This worked for my mother as well as for me. As soon as I realized that my mother was gone I lost my purpose. I was just blowing steam into the wind while she was outside feeling much less controlled by my outburst. The simple act of getting up to find her broke the emotional storm.

Of course we cannot always withdraw or expect others to stop their negative thoughts or actions. But we can protect our peace of mind by not entering into negativity and by seeking creative solutions from the positive flow. My mother's inspiration to just walk away was new to her. She had never tried it before. While that might not be the safest solution today, back then it did do the job. In her own way she unconsciously tapped into a positive solution. What we want to do is consciously tap into this potential in all of our life experiences just the way she did spontaneously.

My turmoil in the store has provided many laughs over the years. The recollection of these experiences adds spice to our lives, so we shouldn't see life challenges as all bad. They are the very experiences that will eventually lead us to freedom in Spirit.

It is helpful to understand that our predilection to emote in any given way can be exacerbated by chemical changes in the body. We are living through a physical form that, just like an old jalopy, can have quirks and idiosyncrasies that we will need to be aware of and to nurture from time to time. Examples of biologically based challenges can be different types of mental illness, reactions to sugar or other foods, menopause and premenstrual syndrome. Tuning into the physiology of our bodies and working practically with these physical plane issues will help to bring our emotions into balance.

This is another reason to develop honest introspection. When we get to know ourselves well we will be able to tell more easily where our emotions are coming from. That understanding will help us to develop a positive relationship with the physcial form life has provided us to grow through.

Keep in mind that we are not our emotions. They are simply the outward fluctuations of the ego/personality that we have become identified with. The more that we identify with our inner self beyond the emotions the less power emotions will have over us.

Affirmations are a powerful way to redirect your emotions. When you feel strong negative emotions trying to take hold of you choose a phrase that reflects a positive mental quality and repeat it with intense concentration.

For example: If you feel yourself getting mentally agitated you might affirm: "Calmness is my friend. I am calm. Peace fills and surrounds me." If you are feeling sad you might affirm: "I release all sorrow into the ocean of joy. I have come from joy. I return to joy. I am joy, joy, joy."

You can create your own affirmations just by attuning yourself to the positive flow. The unique combination of ideas that are suited to your personal needs will often present themselves. It is fun, creative and it works!

Meditation is also a powerful way to redirect your attention from emotion consciousness to inner peace consciousness.

The releasing of negative emotions is a challenge for everyone who has them - which is almost everyone! Use our formula to explore what works for you. Observe your mental landscape without judgment. Root your awareness in the positive flow. The feelings that you receive from the positive flow will not be the same as your emotional feelings. They are rooted in a calmness that does not fluctuate like the emotions. Over time you will discern the difference. Inwardly seek creative solutions and then experiment with your inspirations.

True happiness is not a roller coaster of exciting ups and depressing downs that come as a result of outward experiences. True happiness is a deep state of well-being that comes from our inner connection to the infinite joy of Spirit.

Chapter 19
Three Keys to Success

The principles that we have been discussing are central to all life experiences. The negative flow wants us to dwell on the differences in life; like in war "Divide and conquer" is its motto. The truths of the positive flow however are based on the unity of all life. Even though things look separate and different on the outside all of life is unified on the inside. So the basis for attaining success in life is the same no matter in which area of life we are trying to succeed.

Once you have attuned yourself to a direction in life you will need to apply energy, concentration and determination in order to succeed. These three components are the essential to success inwardly and outwardly.

Energy

Nothing happens in life without energy. It takes energy to digest your food, think a thought, experience an emotion, watch a sunset or listen to music. Virtually everything in life takes energy. At the same time, one of the laws of physics says that energy cannot be created or destroyed. So where does energy come from and where does it go after being used? And how can we tap into the volume of energy that we will need for success in life?

Energy flows into the physical world through the more subtle astral world. We touched on this in Chapter Two. All of life is inwardly animated from the universal storehouse of energy. Energy, like all of life, is a flow; it isn't stationary. So when energy is needed it is drawn in and then released through the energized activity. Once utilized by any given action in life the energy moves on like water down a stream. As long as the creation continues that energy will simply flow through the creation garbed in one form or another.

Many people think that the physical body is powered by food. It is true that the biological processes of the body do include the use of physical fuels. But the animating power underneath the energy in the food and the ability to process that food is manifest through the underlying powers of Spirit. Certainly it is helpful to eat right and fuel the body with healthful foods. Even more important then food is learning to draw on the energy of the positive flow as an actual force that can be channeled through us to achieve our goals.

Energy powers not only our bodies but our minds as well. The process of thinking and directing our lives takes huge amounts of energy. In order to increase our chances of success in any mental or physical activity we need to bring as much energy to bear on our goal as possible.

It has been said that the difference between great athletes and average or just good athletes is "heart". Heart in this context is the connection of an indomitable spirit to the inner wellspring of universal potential; or energy. We can consciously connect ourselves with this limitless power through the channel of our will.

Try this experiment.

Make a fist. Now tense the muscles in your hand. Tighten your fist as much as you can. Is it tightened all of the way? Yes? Try to make it tighter. Is it tight as you can now? Tighten it more...Now relax your hand and move your fingers around to help release the energy.

If you really do this experiment you will find that there is no point at which you cannot tighten your fist just a little bit harder. If you had sufficient concentration and determination you could literally tear the flesh off your hand. While that is not a particularly useful ability in itself, it is helpful as an example for understanding that energy comes from within through our will and that it has no limit.

Jesus said, "If ye had but faith ye could move mountains." An aspect of what he was referring to is this principle of application of will. If we learn to channel the energy of the universe through our will there are few limits to what we can accomplish.

Concentration

Now that we understand we must channel energy through our will in the direction of our goals we come to the next key to success: Concentration. Concentration is the focusing of our energy through our will.

We've all met people who have lots of energy but never get anything done. That is because they have not learned to focus their energies. We even describe people like this as being mentally scattered. It doesn't matter how much potential we have if we never learn to focus that potential and manifest results. Deep concentratioin will give us the ability to bring ever increasing amounts of energy to bear on any physical or mental task that we face in life.

Concentration is also the key to meditation and to developing our connection to the positive flow. Many people think that meditation is just a passive form of mental relaxation. Deep meditation is the intense (but relaxed) focusing of the mind inwardly to perceive our inner connection to Spirit. Just the way a radio must be tuned to a specific channel to receive a signal so it is that the mind must be focused with clarity and single pointed intensity to discern the more subtle realms of Spirit.

Determination

Once we develop the ability to concentrate, our success in any endeavor is simply (but not always easily) an issue of duration or determination. When we really want something we simply cannot give up until we get it. Isn't that what inspires us about the lives of others who have achieved great accomplishments? It is thrilling to hear about how someone has overcome all obstacles, defying all the odds and the opinions of the "experts" to rise triumphantly atop the goal that they set for themselves.

Our Spirits rise inwardly in sympathetic harmony with the successes of others. We instinctively know that we too can rise to that kind of success as expressed through our own lives. This is one of the benefits of spending time in the presence of people who are successful in the way we want to be successful. They will inspire and magnetize us towards our own success.

How long it will take to achieve success in any task that we set or find before us is not often known to us. We cannot say for sure when we will reach the top of the mountain that we have chosen to climb. But we do know that getting to the top is dependent on how much energy we bring to bear on our goal, how well we concentrate that energy and how determined we are to achieve our goal.

Experiment with ways that you can apply these ideas in your own life. Start with modest tasks while you learn to use your tools of energy, concentration and determination. Then as you become stronger in your practice choose ever higher goals. Let your connection to the positive flow be your guide. While you accomplish your outward goals in life, don't forget that the greatest achievement is your complete awakening in the source of the positive flow: Infinite Spirit.

Chapter 20
Heroes, Coaches, Mentors and Spiritual Guides

Over the years I have heard the results of many polls that list the names of people who are most admired for their accomplishments in life. Invariably you find the names of movie stars, rock stars, professional athletes and well-known politicians. These people are held up to children and society in general as the peak of human achievement.

The way of the world is to promote that which is most outwardly exciting. The World Series in baseball is exciting. The man who hits in the winning run is a hero! The National Football League's championship game the Superbowl is one of the biggest events in the world every year. The man who makes most valuable player in that game is set for life! The Indy 500 car race, the Kentucky Derby, national rock concert tours, television shows and movies, these are the great events and performances of our time. The winners and performers of these events are the heroes of our society. They are emulated and sometimes all but worshiped by our youth. Are these examples the best that we can aspire to? The best we have to offer future generations?

I am not suggesting that there is anything inherently bad or wrong with any of these areas of endeavor. The real issue is not sports or singing, but the qualities of consciousness expressed by human achievement that we want to hold up to ourselves and to our children. We have talked about how all of life expresses elevating, activating or downward-pulling qualities of consciousness. If we want to expand our consciousness and uplift our lives we need to associate with and emulate people, places and things that express upward-flowing vibrations.

Simply put: The ego wants to be a rock star, the soul wants to emulate the saints. The soul doesn't want to be a "saint". It is not about any kind of label or outward recognition; truly holy people seek anonymity unless inwardly guided to do otherwise. It is about being 100% consciously connected to Spirit with no risk of losing that connection. That is the only lasting goal that can be achieved in life, every other achievement is temporary. Oneness with Spirit is the only measure of lasting happiness and ultimate success. It is the true underlying purpose of our existence.

While we advance spiritually there will be many intermediate goals along the way. Some of these goals will be for outward success. There are few activities in life that have no potential benefit to us. The key is to remember that it is our inner growth that measures our success and not the specifics of our outward accomplishments. All endeavors in life are worthwhile to the extent that they help us to express our spiritual nature.

One of the things that we want to keep in mind is that the results of our associations and actions are often predictable. As I mentioned earlier, environment is almost always stronger than will. So if you spend your time with people who express qualities associated with the negative flow they are invariably going to rub off on you. Likewise, if you associate with positive energies you will increase your own positive energies as well.

We can use this principle to our advantage by choosing our associates consciously. Open yourself up inwardly to feeling how you are vibrationally affected by others. Rather than judging them, apply your powers of discrimination and attunement to the positive flow to evaluate where and with whom you want to spend your time.

Way of the Positive Flow

It is interesting that people who are serious about improving their skills in any outward endeavor will not hesitate to find a teacher, coach or mentor. But when it comes to perfecting oneself on the inside many people are resistant to seek help. The negative flow feeds people thoughts like, "No one 'really' knows about this stuff. No one is going to get between me and God. I can find my own way!" This way of thinking causes many people to wander aimlessly through this world. Yet few people would hesitate to ask for a map or a guide when traveling in a foreign country. They wouldn't question the instructions of a world famous golfer on how to hit the ball properly. The guidance of a famous ballerina on proper toe technique would be readily accepted and appreciated by most students.

Admittedly it is easier to gauge a person's golfing or dancing abilities than to discern their level of spiritual development. It is also true that spiritual matters penetrate to inner levels of being that we would not necessarily share with a sports or academic coach. The solution to this dilemma is to develop our understanding about spiritual matters, not to isolate ourselves from help that is not only greatly beneficial, but at times essential.

Many people think that they need to choose a spiritual path. The reality is that all of life is itself the spiritual path. Our inner connection to the positive flow, Spirit, God, or whatever else you want to call it, is the only point of personal communication that we can have with the universe. Having said that, it is also true that we will have to make some practical choices in order to grow spiritually.

The first choice we need to make is that we truly want to grow spiritually. Until we make that decision we will be a rudderless student of life. The boat of our spiritual growth will wander according to the winds of the world. Having decided that we want to know more about how life works one of two things will happen. Life will either present a spiritual opportunity to us or we will start generally searching about like a puppy dog looking for a home. Some people read books. Others take classes. There is not just one way that people find their personal spiritual path. The thing to remember is that the more energy we put out to gain understanding about life the greater will be our magnetism to draw a response.

Each of us has different preferences when it comes to style. While it is true that we will eventually grow beyond outward style, we need to get started with something that feels comfortable to us. The first direction that we choose may or may not be the long term path that best suits our needs. Paying attention to how we feel inwardly is the only reliable way to tell if we are headed in the right direction.

What we are all trying to find is our spiritual family: A way of approaching Spirit, style of expression and a group of like-minded people that feels like home to us. Finding your spiritual family is one of the greatest blessings in the spiritual life. It isn't just a question of continuous attendance at the same place of worship. Some people go to the same church for their whole life and never truly feel what I am talking about. Imagine having a very happy childhood and then going away from your family and friends for a long, long time. The feeling of positive homecoming that you would have upon returning would be akin to what I am trying to describe.

A practical approach to finding your spiritual family is to use your connection to the positive flow. After you have spent some time in meditation, focus your attention at the spiritual eye. Broadcast from that point out into the universe your desire to find your spiritual family. We talked about how to do this in Chapter Ten - Creativity and Materializing your Dreams. Refer back to that chapter as a reminder.

Another aspect of this has to do with spiritual guides. This can be a touchy subject because many people are hyper-aware of the misdeeds of people who have represented themselves as being more spiritual than they apparently were.

Way of the Positive Flow

Certainly no one wants to get caught up in a storm of negative energies. Especially when it is associated with something so dear and close as our spiritual lives. At the same time, if you want to look at sheer numbers of opportunities to have unpleasant experiences, life is full of them. Every school has some poor teachers. Almost every office has at least one mean-spirited worker. There are coaches and instructors in all life endeavors who misuse their positions in some way. The fact is that this world is not a very safe place to avoid being hurt or misused. We do not let these risks stop us from flying in airplanes, driving down the street or learning to play the piano. Let's not use this as an excuse to avoid growing in our relationship with the only truly safe place in life: Spirit.

People do not seem to mind as much if their swimming or football coach isn't perfect. Most coaches berate their students, and some have been known to get physical with them. But when a spiritual leader is not perfect people become deeply offended. For some reason people think that the label priest, minister, monk or nun means that a person has achieved their spiritual goal. It is common to think that people in those positions should be held to a higher standard than others. While it is true that they may be consciously aspiring to a higher standard, attempting and succeeding are not the same thing. Maybe churches should be forced to post a public notice: Parishioners beware, our leaders are not perfect!

The universe holds all souls to the same standard. If it were otherwise then there would be no such thing as cosmic law or universal truth. Without universal laws, chaos would reign, spirituality would not exist and there would be no purpose to life. Actually, the idea that life has no ultimate purpose and that God does not exist is a point of view that the negative flow tries to plant in the mind. Fortunately it does not hold water for long. The soul knows instinctively that life is good and that God does exist. Opposing that truth can only be a temporary point of view.

Heroes, Coaches, Mentors & Spiritual Guides

The real problem is that many spiritual groups and their leaders promote themselves as being better than others. They advertise that they are blessed with secret knowledge and understanding. In extreme cases they claim that they are infallible as well. There is little the spiritual neophyte can do to verify claims of spiritual infallibility.

Historically this has been a challenge from time immemorial; it is not unique to our times. Increased population and the ease of communications have created a general public that is much more aware of these situations when they arise. What we need to do is bring this issue down to a very personal level. Keep in mind that there is not just one right way of looking at these issues. Our goal is to find a resolution that resonates with our own understanding of truth. This is why having a personal relationship with the positive flow is so powerful.

Please don't misunderstand me: I am not suggesting that we should make truth fit our view of it. What we need to do is raise ourselves up so that when we meet the truth in our lives we will, through our inner connection to the positive flow, recognize it.

Most spiritual leaders are not perfect. Yet we all will need a spiritual guide at some point along the path. How do we reconcile this? The key is to understand that we do not need a perfect teacher. What we need is the perfect teacher for us. We can always hope that the perfect teacher for us will be a perfect teacher - fully self-realized - but don't count on it.

As students we simply do not have the apparatus to fully recognize a perfected being. If we met Jesus Christ or Buddha on the street would we be able to recognize them as perfected beings? Since most people didn't when they had the opportunity back in those times we can infer that things would probably be the same now. As a practical matter, in the highest sense, it takes one to truly know one.

What we can do at this time is to cultivate our inner connection to Spirit so that we are more able to recognize the vibrations of others. Gradually we will refine our inner connection to the perception of these vibrations so that when we meet higher beings, or maybe even a perfected being, we will be more able to recognize them as such.

Another thing to keep in mind is that while it is a fantastic blessing and spiritual opportunity to be in the presence of a self-realized being, it is also incredibly demanding. When you spend time with the big leaguers in any field of endeavor you have to constantly stretch yourself to higher levels of performance. Imagine living in the presence of a being that can know every thought and motivation that crosses through your mind. At least God is invisible to us! The saints stand before us to remind us of our potential, but inevitably, they also remind us of our shortcomings.

The positive flow is so sensitive to our needs that we are constantly being given the right thing at the right time for our life. If our lives are not progressing the way we would like, what we need to do is change the qualities of energy that we are putting out. That will change our magnetism. Our new energies will draw new results. The use of this principle should be applied to drawing the right teacher for each of us.

It is said in India that when we have put out the sufficent amount of energy in the direction of returning to our home in Spirit, God chooses a spiritual guide for us. Our personal guide's goal is not to control us in any way but to help free us from the limitations of this world. This spiritual guide is called a guru. The true guru is a perfected being that has become vibrationally connected to us. Our guru commits to helping us become free from limitation no matter how long it takes - even through multiple incarnations.

We can have many teachers, coaches and mentors - call them what you will - but only one true guru. A guru is an individualized expression of Spirit just like you and I. The difference is that a true guru has transcended that individuality and become fully identified with the ocean of Spirit.

Heroes, Coaches, Mentors & Spiritual Guides

A fully realized being like this is called a master. Not a master of others but a master of their own self. Teachers who seek power over others are not fully realized beings. A master has no ego driven desires. True teachers in all fields of endeavor do not seek to control their students but to inspire them to new heights. Great teachers have the insight to bring out the best in their students. Each student is unique and tapping into that uniqueness is central to the kind of personalized guidance that is necessary for higher education.

Our true guru is able to work with us without regard to time and space. Through the laws of magnetism the guru affects us internally with uplifting energies. Outward instructions and even physical presence are helpful but quite secondary to this process. The key to success in our relationship with the guru is to first magnetically attract a guru and then to increase our awareness of the guru's presence in our lives through our connection to the positive flow. This inner attunement is where the transformation of our consciousness actually takes place.

How this guru/disciple relationship manifests in this world at this time for each of us is individual. If your true guru is currently animating a form in this world you may or may not be able to actually spend time with him or her. If your guru is not in the body (and often even if they are) they will most certainly send help to you through various representatives. These souls are not always aware that they have been internally guided to help you in some way. Elder disciples, depending on the strength of their inner connection to Spirit, are natural resources for younger disciples.

Help in the spiritual life can come from a person on a completely different outward path as well. True teachers are not jealous about how, where or when you get help. At the same time remember one of the great laws of the spiritual life: loyalty.

We should not enter lightly into what is perceived as a guru/disciple relationship. Once that bond is forged we lose much of our forward spiritual momentum by breaking that bond. Spiritual divorce has repercussions that are even stronger than matrimonial divorce.

Always keep in mind that no mistake or difficulty in the spiritual life is a game breaker. We can never be forever lost or eternally cast into some kind of hell. Through our inner connection to the positive flow the chances of being misled are greatly diminished. Even so, we will all make mistakes and suffer the consequences of those mistakes. That is how we grow. As long as we continue to pick ourselves up and take step after step along the journey, we will eventually arrive at our goal. It is far better to commit ourselves to a lesser teacher and experience the turmoil of discovering that they are not right for us than to stand on the sidelines and be a watcher instead of a player.

A true guru is the greatest gift that a sincere seeker can receive. The guru is not only proof that God has heard your prayer, but a level of support that means you have a realistic chance of making substantial progress in this lifetime. If you want to hasten your spiritual progress, inwardly connect yourself to the positive flow and broadcast intensely with deep sincerity your desire to find your spiritual guide and path.

Chapter 21
10 Tricks
of the Trade

Craftsmen in all areas of life learn over the years that there are little tricks of the trade that can make life easier and increase the effectiveness of their efforts. I hope these ideas will be as helpful for you as they have been for me. If they seem simple or obvious, keep in mind that it is often the simplest things in life that actually work …that is, once we know about them.

1. Truisms in life have meanings that we can explore to reach new levels of understanding as long as we don't get the false idea that we already know it all. Practice humility and seek to understand ever deeper levels of truth.

2. Silence is the doorway through which we perceive truth. Practice living in the stillness that lays beneath the tumultuous surface of all life. This is where we can find peace and discover truth.

3. Deep meditation is the most vibrationally trans-forming activity that we can engage in to raise our consciousness and release ourselves from the past. It may not look like much from the outside, but on the inside it is the forge in which we can smith the awakening of our awareness from the limits of the body/mind/ego to our true Self as Infinite Spirit.

4. Next to having a guru and the ability to meditate deeply, spiritual fellowship is the greatest blessing in the

147

spiritual life. In India they call this fellowship satsang. Satsang means fellowship with truth. This is not the truth of "my way is the only way," it is the truth of life itself as experienced through our connection to the positive flow. Satsang is an inner state of consciousness that can be experienced when we spend time in an uplifting environment with other like-minded souls. The group magnetism is much more powerful than our own efforts by themselves. When you are just getting started and you cannot yet meditate very well satsang will magnetize you internally and help you to feel inwardly connected. Even experienced travelers on the spiritual path will find that satsang with those who share their spiritual aspirations will greatly enhance their lives.

5. Be a giver in life. Those who are givers by nature or develop it through practice live happier lives. They also expand their sympathies beyond personal ego concerns. Giving helps to free us from the "I and mine" consciousness that is associated with the negative flow. Even though giving is almost always good, if we give with ego we can lose our internal balance. The key is to spontaneously give through our inspirations from the positive flow. Be a conscious channel for beneficial energies to flow into this world.

There are many ways in which to give. For example, we can offer money, time, compassion, a helping hand, a kind thought or a loving prayer. The value of our giving should not be dependent on how it is received. People who give with the thought of what they will get in return, including being thanked, have merchant consciousness not the joy of giving. Seek through your inner connection to the positive flow for invisible opportunities to have giving energies flow through you.

6. Exercise and eat according to the needs of your particular body and lifestyle. Find a balanced regime that feels right to you and then give your attention to other areas of improvement. No amount of health food or exercise is going to take the place of doing your internal homework. Spiritual

success comes from the transformation of the soul, not the rippling of stomach muscles or a properly formulated power shake.

7. Try to avoid the phenomenal side of the spiritual life. Visions, psychic readings and astral travel are all possible. They are even helpful at times. But they tend to give the impression that the spiritual life is a side show. If they remind us that the underlying energies in life are real and useful to us then okay. If we think that reading tarot cards is going to help us the same way that a regular practice of mediation will, we are not seeing things clearly.

Astrology is another part of this area that can sidetrack people. It is far easier to have your chart read or learn to read a chart than it is to transform your consciousness through spiritual practices. Astrologers, card readers and psychics are ranked in the thousands but just like spiritual guides, truly wise practitioners are far and few between. If you feel guided by the positive flow to explore these areas of interest then by all means do so; just don't let them distract you from developing a genuine personal relationship with Spirit.

8. Once you find a style of spiritual practice that feels like home, enter into it fully and stick with it. Give it a fair chance to help you. Many people move on to another style before they have given their current path a chance to work. Certainly you must follow your inner guidance, but as a general guideline, don't give up on your practice unless you receive a strong inner inspiration. If it is time to move on do so with dignity and grace. Try not to leave on a negative note. Be thankful for the good that you have received.

9. Respect others at all times and in all circumstances. No matter how dim the light may be Spirit is shining at the foundation of all people. This does not mean we agree with all of their choices. What we respect is the freedom that each soul has to make its own decisions. Even if we have to take a stand against another person or group, we must never give in to hate.

Way of the Positive Flow

When we feel hate we are connecting to the negative flow and are diminishing the light that is trying to shine through our lives.

10. God is always present. God loves us more than we know. God is never mad at us. Transcend your thoughts and emotions; live in the vastness of universal love that flows through your heart center. While you are in there looking around, give God a hug!

Chapter 22
Riding the Wave
of Your Life

Throughout my many years of surfing I always dreamed of riding the ultimate wave. I dreamed of being in the right place at the right time to catch the greatest wave of my life. Little did I know that the greatest wave would not be a wave in the ocean, but the wave of life itself.

Of course, riding the ultimate wave isn't as simple as walking down the road. The wave that I was dreaming of riding was huge. If I was going to get the thrill of my life I knew it had to be the biggest wave of my life. The only problem is that big waves are really scary! Great accomplishments in life often include conquering our fears in some way. It is not just a question of facing the fear of injury or physical death, it could also be the fear of failure or embarrassment.

People's fears come in many shades and colors. The thing to remember is that we all have them in one form or another, and we all need to work through those fears if we want to succeed at our chosen dream.

When I remember the biggest wave I ever rode, which was almost four times as tall as me, I do not think so much of the ride as the fact that I actually was out there in the ocean facing the big ones. Stepping up to the plate and facing the challenge of our goals is the only way to actually achieve them. Don't just sit up in the stands watching others go after their dreams. No matter what path you choose in life, step up to the plate, face your fears and give it your best shot.

My biggest ride was also the biggest wipeout thahad. I always knew I could survive riding a big wave. What I did not know is if I could survive wiping out on such a big wave. It took me about 40 minutes to reach the beach after being completely thrashed by countless walls of water on my swim in. My surfboard was washed out to sea and never seen again. When I finally got to the shore and stood safely on the sand looking out at the waves, I realized that I had survived: I was grinning from ear to ear.

If I had accidentally fallen out of a boat and had to survive the waves in order to get to shore my experience would have been very different. The same challenge of survival would have a completely different meaning to me. The key difference is that I chose consciously to go out into the waves. This act of conscious volition is essential. In order to achieve ever deeper levels of attunement with the positive flow of life we need to consciously enter into the relationship. It is our choice.

We have talked a lot about how to make choices through attunement to the positive flow. As you work with this inner guidance be sure to add a good measure of common sense. While I was inspired to go surfing that day the waves were so big, I was not unprepared. I had been surfing for many years and had much experience in the water.

On another occasion a friend of mine and I found a surf spot that we had never seen before. The shape of the waves were fantastic. There were no other surfers around to compete with us for the waves. It was the perfect opportunity to surf. Fortunately we took the time to sit on the shore and watch the waves for a while before we paddled out.

The waves were big but they looked rideable. As we watched wave after wave come in we could just imagine the incredible rides that we would have. We started to get ready to go out when our eyes were drawn out to sea by huge mountains of ocean that were making their way in towards the shore. We had estimated that the waves were coming in around four to five times as tall as a person. These new waves were much bigger. We estimated them at over six times as tall as a person, they were huge.

We watched those waves for a long time. They all looked perfectly rideable. They were wonderful to see. Oh, how we wanted to ride those waves. Even so, deep down inside we knew that they were too big for us. That day we stayed humbly on the beach.

Be courageous in life, but do not be foolish. Use your common sense. Basic precepts like: Look before you leap! never go out of style.

When riding waves the ultimate experience is to be completely inside the curl of the wave. It is called being in the tube. When you are inside the wave people on shore cannot see you. The roar of the wave fills your ears. When you come shooting out the end it's like being reborn into the world. Your senses are sharp and fresh, adrenaline is flowing through your viens and you feel energetically alive.

This kind of peak outward experience is what all sportsmen are seeking. When people say that their sport is best, what they are really saying is that this feeling of exhilaration is the best. This same analogy works in the spiritual life. It doesn't matter what style of religion we follow, it is the inner feeling that we have when we feel connected to Spirit that provides its true value. Those who are inwardly connected through Buddhism are tapping into the same internal truth that Christians, Jews, and Hindus experience. Agnostics and Atheists can all connect to this same internal reality.

In our "scientific" society, most people are amazingly non-scientific in their beliefs. People are all too quick to follow a dogma than to demand their own internal proof. Science is based on personally verifiable experiments. Everything that we have talked about is personally verifiable by you.

Way of the Positive Flow

We are all challenged each day to wake up and live well. Imagine looking back on the very last day of your life and surveying all that you have accomplished. What will it look like? For each of us the details will be different, but the essence will be the same: How much do we grow our spirit? How much joy and love did we share? These are the bench marks of a good life.

Utilize the principles that we have discussed to transform your life. These truths have an incredible power to improve our lives, but we must activate that power by consciously entering into the process. It is not enough to believe that these ideas may be true or to even agree with them fully, we must act in order to manifest positive changes in our lives.

For those with doubts that these precepts will be helpful, no problem! Good natured skepticism is healthy - it keeps the mind sharp. At the same time, negative skepticism can keep us from exploring areas of life that we would find very beneficial if we would just open ourselves up to new possibilities. This is one of the ways that the negative flow tries to keep us tied to a limited view of life. In this case, from the very beginning I have encouraged you not to take my word for it but to experience it for yourself through your own experiments in life. Once again: The choice is yours.

There is no limit to what we can accomplish spiritually in this lifetime. Through the practice of the principles that we have discussed and the direct perception of Spirit in deep meditation we can reunite the wave of our individualized consciousness with the ocean of infinite ever-new joy that is often called God. This is our potential if we choose it.

It is my heartfelt prayer that the love, joy and wisdom of the positive flow will grow strong in your life and that you will, like myself, have the joy of sharing it with others.

So, now you know what to do!

More books
by Lawrence Vijay Girard
(Nayaswami Vijay)

Meditation
The Science and Art of Stillness

Positive Flow Parenting

Flowing in the Workplace
A Guide to Personal and
Professional Success

Doorway to a New Lifetime
Childbirth from a Spiritual View

The Journey of Discipleship
Book 1 - Traveling with Swamiji

The Adventures of
Harry Fruitgarden
Series

Book 1 - What's it All About?
Book 2 - Who Would Have Guessed?

Ask us about
Positive Flow Seminars
with Lawrence Vijay Girard
(Nayaswami Vijay)

---

www.FruitgardenPublishing.com